Night Watch

night watch

by Lucille Fletcher

Random House : New York

Library of Congress Cataloging in Publication Data

Fletcher, Lucille.
Night watch.

I. Title.
PS3556.L424N5   813'.5'4   72–6664
ISBN 0–394–48258–1

Manufactured in the United States of America by Haddon Craftsmen, Scranton, Pennsylvania.

NIGHT WATCH *was first presented on February 28, 1972, by George W. George and Barnard S. Straus at the Morosco Theatre in New York City with the following cast:*

(In order of appearance)

ELAINE WHEELER	Joan Hackett
JOHN WHEELER	Len Cariou
HELGA	Jeanne Hepple
VANELLI	Martin Shakar
CURTIS APPLEBY	Keene Curtis
BLANCHE COOKE	Elaine Kerr
LIEUTENANT WALKER	William Kiehl
DR. TRACEY LAKE	Barbara Cason
SAM HOKE	Rudy Bond

The Scene

The action takes place in the library of a townhouse in New York's East Thirties. The time is the present.

Act One

Scene One: A winter morning, five o'clock
Scene Two: The same day, five o'clock in the evening

Act Two

Scene One: Twenty minutes later
Scene Two: Three days later, nine o'clock in the evening

ACT ONE

It is five o'clock of a winter morning in New York City. The curtain rises on a dimly lit room, faintly illuminated by moonlight. It is the beautifully furnished· library or back drawing-room of a remodeled brownstone, complete with paneling and a fireplace. At the extreme left of the stage and at right angles to the proscenium is a large window, the handsome draperies of which are wide apart. We cannot see what lies beyond.

A sofa and a coffee table face this window. Behind the sofa is a long table on which are a lamp, a telephone, ashtrays, a cigarette box. The room also contains an open doorway through which a staircase can be glimpsed, and a small bar equipped with bottles, glasses, etc. There are fine modern paintings on the walls—a Picasso, a Modigliani—bookshelves, and a chess set. At stage right is a handsome wing chair of green velour.

ELAINE WHEELER is seated on the arm of the sofa, smoking a cigarette and dangling a key in her left hand. She is slender, patrician, with big eyes, an eager smile, an air of insecurity. She wears an exquisite long dressing gown.

After a moment or two she rises and moves to the window, jiggling the key, which has a metal tag on it. Softly, desultorily, she hums or sings a few bars of "Frère Jacques." A clock with Westminster chimes begins to strike the hour of five.

As it is striking, a light goes on in the hall, and a man is seen descending the staircase. He is JOHN WHEELER, *handsome, rugged, in his thirties, wearing pajama bottoms and a robe.*

When ELAINE *hears him, she rushes to put out the cigarette and hides the key in the silent butler on the library table. Then quickly she begins to empty the ashtrays and generally tidy up.*

JOHN *(Entering)* Elaine! For God's sake. Do you know what time it is?

ELAINE Oh . . . I'm sorry. Did I wake you, dear?

JOHN No. *(Moving to the coffee table, noticing the cigarette butts, the litter)* You smoked a *pack?* Another one? What's happening to you, Ellie?

ELAINE Me? Nothing . . . I couldn't sleep.
(A little nervous smile)

JOHN Come *on!* It's been three nights in a row. Cigarette butts all over the place . . . Crossword puzzles . . .

ELAINE It's just my old insomnia—it's inherited. Daddy had it. Granddaddy suffered from it. We are night owls, moon people.
(She stands before the window, a graceful figure in the moonlight. He makes a disparaging noise. He

starts moving around the room restlessly—picking up a book, a newspaper)

JOHN   Ellie . . . I've heard all that before . . . *(Slight pause)* What's the problem? Me?

ELAINE   Of course not, darling.

JOHN   I couldn't make it home any earlier for dinner.

ELAINE *(Moving to window and looking out)*   I understood that, dear.

JOHN   It isn't Blanche, is it?

ELAINE   Blanche—?

JOHN   Well—she's beginning to get on *my* nerves . . .

ELAINE *(Smiling—gently)*   She's been nothing but a darling . . . I've loved having her—

JOHN *(Impatiently)*   Then what is it? *(Looking at her)* Insomnia isn't inherited. You've always had a reason . . . *(Slight pause)* Is it Carl? That bastard . . . ?

ELAINE *(Moving to the table, picking up a cigarette)*   C-Carl?

JOHN   Blanche said you'd been talking about him.

ELAINE   That's nonsense. She brought him up. I didn't. *(Lighting a cigarette)* Look, you're a day person and I'm a night person. When you go to bed, you fall asleep like

that. But I—well, sometimes—the very minute my head touches the pillow, right away the candles light up. The music begins. And I'm a girl in crinoline standing at the entrance to a gorgeous ballroom . . . But I can't go to a ball obviously . . .
(Smiling, she pirouettes)

JOHN *(Turning away, bored)* Okay . . . okay. *(Turning to* ELAINE, *shaking his head)* Something's got to be done about you, Ellie . . .

ELAINE *(Lightly—gaily)* What? Just bundle me off to Switzerland?

JOHN Well, why not try it? Nothing else seems to work. It could be a—vacation. *(She smiles)* What's so funny?

ELAINE *(Smiling)* You. You need a vacation, darling. *(Slight pause)* Please. Stop prowling around. I'm perfectly all right.

JOHN Then what is it?

ELAINE Nothing, absolutely nothing. Don't make so much of it—really, dear. I'll end up thinking I'm some sort of freak.
(Half smiling, she clowns a little, acting the part of someone slightly addled)

JOHN Oh, the hell with it, Ellie . . . *(He strides toward the door)*

ELAINE *(Quickly, appeasing)* John, darling, you're tired, I'm tired. But if there's something you want to talk about . . . anything special . . . then let's just stay down here for a little while together. I'll make some coffee, like the old days. And I won't smoke. *(She puts out cigarette)* It might help—both of us . . .

JOHN *(Looking at her a second, then turning away)* I'm sorry . . . but it's late, and I'm hungry, if you don't mind —*(Moving to the door)* That was a pretty lousy dinner Helga cooked up tonight.

ELAINE I thought you were dieting . . .

JOHN Care for anything? Glass of milk maybe?

ELAINE No thanks.

JOHN *(Leaving)* Well, I'm starved.

ELAINE John . . . *(He stops. Intensely)* Hold me . . . please.

JOHN *(Looking at her, frowning)* Ellie . . . *(He moves toward her slowly, takes her in his arms)* What the hell is the matter with you? You're like ice. You're shaking. Here—put this over you. *(He picks up the coverlet and puts it around her. He moves to the hall, pauses)* Who the hell's been fooling with this thermostat?
(He exits. She stands there looking after him forlornly, wrapped in the coverlet. She shivers. Then, walking toward the window, she mechanically picks up a cigarette and a matchbook. As she is about to

7

light the cigarette, her eye is suddenly caught as though by something out the window. She moves hastily to the window. She screams a bloodcurdling scream, dropping the unlit cigarette and matchbook)

ELAINE *(Looking toward the door)* John! John—will you come up here? Please. Right away, please! *John! (There is no answer. She whirls back to the window again. She stares frozen, her expression registering horror. Then she totters forward, grabbing for the draperies, which rip. She screams, moving to the door)* John! John, will you please come up here? John! JOHN!
(She registers babbling terror and hysteria. JOHN *enters. She clutches him)*

JOHN   Now, what in God's name! . . . What is it? What's the matter?

ELAINE *(Clutching him hysterically)*   Oh, John, oh, John, it's horrible! It's horrible!

JOHN   What? What is?

ELAINE *(Burying her head against him)*   Just look out that window, please. It's—it's hideous.
*(*JOHN *detaches himself and walks to the window. He looks out)*

JOHN   What in hell are you talking about?

ELAINE *(Coming toward him)* Right across . . . where the shade's up . . . *(She freezes, stares aghast)* Oh, my God. They've pulled it down. Did you see it? Didn't you see it?

JOHN What?

ELAINE A—dead man . . . He was sitting there with his eyes wide open. Dead. Dead. Dead.

JOHN Oh, my God, what kind of crazy—

ELAINE *(Emotionally)* He was there, John. The shade went up just as I was lighting a cigarette. I saw him. Just sitting there. His head was all loose and wobbly, his eyes were fixed. They had this glassy stare. They were looking at me.

JOHN *(Moving to her)* Now, wait a minute, wait a minute. This is wild. How do you know the man was dead?

ELAINE Well, I've seen dead people before. He was bleeding.

JOHN Bleeding? From where?

ELAINE His mouth. There was this trickle of blood like a dark snake in the moonlight. I grabbed the drapes . . . *(Moving toward the phone)* I'm going to call the police. We've got to right away . . .

JOHN *(Hastily turning on some lights and moving to her)* No, wait a second. Take it easy. Let's not get carried away.

(He intercepts her phoning) I'm perfectly willing to call, but let's get some things straight.
(He takes the phone away from her)

ELAINE John, we can't be like those people in the newspapers who watch people murdered outside their windows.

JOHN You're sure he wasn't an illusion? The moonlight or shadows—?

ELAINE *(Vehemently)* He was perfectly real! *(Moving to the window)* That shade's never moved in all the months we've been here. *(Moving to* JOHN *tensely)* Oh, please, let's call. We're wasting time. Those people will get away.

JOHN *(After studying her for a second)* How old was this man?

ELAINE Oh—middle-aged. And his hair looked sort of silvery in the moonlight. He was sitting in a big wing chair.

JOHN A wing chair?

ELAINE *(Moving toward the wing chair in her library)* Yes, definitely. I could see the arms and the high curved back. *(Indicating the chair)* Like that one, sort of. Only not of velour . . . some sort of green brocade material.

JOHN Green brocade! At that distance?

ELAINE It's not that far away. I notice such things. Let's call. Why won't you call?
(Her voice rises to a pitch of tension)

JOHN *(Looking at her for one more second)* Okay, okay. *(He picks up the phone and dials the police number 9– 1–1.* ELAINE *picks up another cigarette and lights it. She paces up and down in front of the window)* Hello. I'm calling to report a body, a dead body. My address? The Kips Bay district. 316 East Thirtieth Street. Manhattan. Wheeler. John Wheeler.

ELAINE *(Half to herself)* All slumped down with his head back, staring at me, with those glassy eyes.

JOHN Hello. My name is John Wheeler. I live in Manhattan on East Thirtieth Street. And my wife thinks—

ELAINE Thinks, John! I saw him.

JOHN —she's just seen a man's dead body in a building opposite the rear of our house. *(Slight pause)* Look. Can't we get on with it, Sergeant?

ELAINE What's he saying?

JOHN Ellie, relax. He's getting me Homicide . . . *(*ELAINE *sighs. She walks to the window. From behind both* JOHN *and* ELAINE, *unseen by both, we see* HELGA, *the German maid, peering in from the hallway. She wears a bathrobe and hair-curlers. She listens to* JOHN's *phone call)* Hello. HELLO. Oh, sorry. My name is Wheeler, Lieutenant. 316 East Thirtieth Street. Manhattan. I'm calling to report what may have been a murder . . . At least my wife says she saw this dead man in a tenement window—an abandoned tenement facing the rear of our house. He was sitting in a chair . . .

ELAINE   A green wing chair.

JOHN   A green wing chair. Bleeding from the mouth . . . a middle-aged man. What? No, not now. *(ELAINE again moves to the window)* The shade's down. Yeah. No. My wife said the shade was up, and then it went down. Come on, Lieutenant . . . *(HELGA tiptoes away, out of sight)* That's what my wife says, and she's very, very sure. *(Slight pause)* Wheeler. W-H-E-E-L-E-R. 316 East Thirtieth Street . . . Yes. That'd put it on Twenty-ninth Street, middle of the block . . . Right . . . I'm on Wall Street . . . Securities . . . Securities . . . What? . . . Yes . . . Right . . . Got it. Okay, well, thanks a lot. *(He hangs up)* Sonsabitches.

ELAINE   Is he sending somebody?

JOHN   Yes, but you'd think *we'd* committed a crime. Some cop's coming here to talk to us.

ELAINE   Here? But it happened over there!

JOHN   Ellie, I don't run the police department. They send somebody here—they send somebody there. *(Moving to door)* Hell, I'd better get some pants on. *(He exits)* Just take it easy, huh?
     (ELAINE looks after him nervously, then moves to the window. HELGA enters)

HELGA   Madame. A dead man. *Gott in Himmel.*

ELAINE   Oh, Helga. You heard? Yes, isn't it horrible?

HELGA *(Shaking her head, moving to the window)*   That's a real disgrace, that building.

ELAINE   You didn't happen to see him?

HELGA   Me? I was sleeping like a baby, yah, till a couple minutes ago. I just got up to—to look at the clock.

ELAINE   Do you know anything about that place at all? Have you ever seen anybody in it—or that shade up?

HELGA *(Vehemently)*   No, madame. Not since I started working for you. I never saw nothing in that dirty old wreck. But then I got my work to do.

ELAINE   What does it look like from the front?

HELGA   You never see it from the front, Madame? *(She notices the sagging draperies, the torn place, examines them curiously)* Why, it's an old junk-heap with a broken-down stoop. Around the corner. In the middle of the block yet, next to a school. And on the other side is a delicatessen—with very bad potato salad that fella makes.

ELAINE   Potato salad?
    (HELGA notices the coverlet in a heap on the floor. She picks it up, strokes it and folds it lovingly)

HELGA   Yah, I wouldn't go into that store again if they shoot me. It's got stale mayonnaise. It upset my digestion. And I heard they robbed that store a coupla times already.

ELAINE *(Nervously)*   Robbed it? *(She moves to the door)* Oh . . . where are the police?

HELGA *(Following her)*   Ach, it's a bad street altogether, that Twenty-ninth Street. With lotsa saloons and plenty filthy foreigners living there. And they got garbage cans and furniture stuck out on the sidewalks—and nasty boys they run after you and pull up your skirt. *(Distant sirens begin. Nodding vehemently; tidying up)* It's a wicked city, madame. It's like war. It's worse than war—with peoples robbing you and stabbing you—for no reason but they just don't like your looks . . . *(JOHN appears, coming down the stairs, dressed in shirt and trousers. He picks up a newspaper from the hallway. To ELAINE, moving toward door)* You like I bring you up your morning chocolate? Or some coffee maybe when I'm dressed?
   (JOHN enters)

JOHN   I'd like some coffee. *(HELGA turns and eyes him coldly)* And a Danish, too, if you don't mind. And that sandwich I was making . . .

HELGA   Oh—so it was *you*—in my kitchen!
   (She exits hastily)

JOHN *(Suppressed fury)*   Ellie!
   (The sirens grow louder. Then die)

ELAINE   I'm sorry. But she works hard—I'll speak to her. *(The doorbell rings)* Here they are. Will you? Shall I? *(She starts for the door)*

JOHN *(Impatiently)*   No. Let *her* go!—for God's sake! *(The front door opens offstage)*

VANELLI *(Offstage; Brooklyn accent)*   This the Wheeler residence?

HELGA *(Offstage)*   Yah . . . *(Shouting)* Mister *Wheeler!* It's the cops!

JOHN *(Exiting)*   I swear she's got the manners of a—a storm trooper!
　　(ELAINE, agitated by all this, looks after him nervously. She glances in a mirror, smoothing her hair. We hear JOHN and VANELLI offstage)

JOHN *(Offstage; smoothly)*   Good morning, Officer. My name is John Wheeler.

VANELLI *(Offstage)*   Morning. You the people who reported a body?

JOHN *(Offstage)*   Yes, we are. My wife's up here.
　　(ELAINE moves toward the door, awaiting their arrival)

VANELLI *(Entering)*   Nice place you got here. You people new in the neighborhood?
　　(He is a nice young Italian cop)

JOHN *(Entering)* We moved in last October. This is Mrs. Wheeler.

VANELLI *(To* ELAINE*)* Mrs. Wheeler? I'm Vanelli, Patrolman Vanelli. Say, is that a real Picasso, ma'am?

ELAINE *(Rather thrown)* Yes, it is. *(She moves to the window)* And this is the window where I saw him . . . the dead man. Right over there—that second-floor window. That shade went up for a minute . . . Is somebody being sent there?

VANELLI Sure, lady. The lieutenant's taking care of it. Nowadays you don't rush any vacant building, unless you're looking to get killed. It takes time, ma'am.

ELAINE *(Nervously)* You can see how close we are . . .

VANELLI *(Peering out)* Yeah. You sure are, I'll say . . . In fact, considering you got that wall there on the right and that left-hand house jutting out so far, it looks like you're the only house on the block can see into those windows.

ELAINE Yes . . . it's rather a cul-de-sac.

VANELLI *(Glancing at her a second)* Yeah? You say this guy was sitting in the window?

ELAINE Yes . . . in a big green wing chair . . .

VANELLI   Yeah? That's funny. I didn't know there was any furniture left in that old dump.

ELAINE   That's strange.

VANELLI   You see, ma'am, around six months ago, they had a fire in there—which practically gutted it. And then the neighborhood kids got in and stole whatever they could lay their hands on.

ELAINE   Well, I know I saw a big green wing chair—sort of like that . . . *(Pointing to the wing chair)* And the man was slouched down into it—like this . . .
(She sits in the wing chair, slumping down, imitating a dead body)

VANELLI *(A grin)*   Say, that's pretty lifelike.

ELAINE   With blood trickling down his face . . . *(Rising)* What else can I tell you? Who owns that building?

VANELLI   God knows, lady, I don't. But it's probably one of those big real-estate combines, they buy up a lotta stuff on what-you-call-it—speculation. *(Moving toward the door)* Okay. We'll see what the story is . . . *(He pauses)* Excuse me, is that a real Modigliani?

ELAINE *(Politely trying to usher him out)*   Yes, it is. You seem to know a great deal about paintings.

VANELLI *(A touch of pride)*   Before I came on the force, I used to be a guard in the Brooklyn Art Museum. And I also took a night course on the subject—which is more than you can say for most guards, right?

ELAINE   Right. You will keep us posted?

VANELLI   Lady, just trust us . . . I hope you got insurance on this stuff?

ELAINE   *(Following him)*   Yes, we do. My husband also keeps a gun handy.

JOHN   *(Under his breath)*   Elaine! *(VANELLI pauses, stares at JOHN)* I have a license for it.

ELAINE   Thank you, Officer.

VANELLI   *(Exiting)*   Likewise. It's a pleasure. *(Glancing around)* Like a museum.

JOHN   Did you have to tell him about that revolver?

ELAINE   What's wrong with owning one? Particularly now? *(Moving to the window)* Why aren't they over there? What's taking all this time?

JOHN   Look, they know what they're doing. *(Studying her, frowning)* You look tired, worn out. Why don't you go upstairs and lie down for a while?

ELAINE   Lie down? When all the excitement is starting?

JOHN   You aren't planning to stay here and run the whole show? *(Still looking at her)* Seriously, Elaine. I've never seen you look so exhausted. Three nights without sleep are raising hell with you, honey . . .

ELAINE *(With a quaver in her tone)* But I can't help not sleeping. It's not my fault!
(The sirens grow louder, closer. She moves to the window. HELGA *enters with a tray)*

HELGA This was all we had in the house, Mr. Wheeler. There was no Danishes.

JOHN *(Coldly)* Yeah?

HELGA *(Taking a cup to* ELAINE *at the window)* Yeah. And I brought for you your morning chocolate, madame. The cops are there already? Good, that's good.

ELAINE *(Peering out)* Perhaps they are, but I can't see anything. *(To* JOHN*)* What do you suppose they're doing over there?

JOHN Who knows? *(To* HELGA*)* Where's Mrs. Cooke?

HELGA *(Rather testily)* I haven't seen her, heard one peep outta her.

JOHN Well, give her a call.

ELAINE *(Turning)* No, don't wake her up, Helga . . . *(To* JOHN, *quickly)* Let the poor child sleep. She's having lunch today with Larry . . . her last date with him. She's breaking it off. And I'm sure she needs all the rest she can get. *(Turning back to the window)* Still no lights. *(There are distant sounds)* But look at all those people running.

Oh, there's that strange-looking man who lives next door
. . . He just came into our yard.

JOHN   What's the matter with his own yard?

ELAINE   He probably couldn't see, with that wall in the way
—*(A sudden gasp)* Oh, there's a light. And another.
*(Lights flicker over the window. The distant commotion
continues)* Two policemen! Three! They're getting in!

JOHN   Take it easy.

ELAINE   *(Crossing to* JOHN, *pulling him to the window)*
Come on. Doesn't it look eerie? Look at that ground
floor . . . those broken beams . . . those naked iron stair-
cases . . .

JOHN   That must have been one hell of a fire . . .

ELAINE   *(Intensely)*   They're going up the stairs! Those
lights! How ghostly! They're coming toward that room!
*(A strong light suddenly illumines their faces. More
distant sounds)*

HELGA   *(Turning suddenly)*   Ach. I don't like dead peoples.
(She exits)

JOHN   *(Trying to draw* ELAINE *away from the window)*   All
right. Come over here. Elaine—

ELAINE   But why? I've seen him. I'm not scared—

JOHN   Come on. Don't try to be so damned courageous. It
could throw you into a tailspin. You know what it could
do. *(As she keeps trying to look out the window, he moves
toward the door)* I'm getting Blanche down here.

ELAINE   Oh, don't be silly. I'm just fine. I'm not going to
do anything . . . I just want to know what happened in
there. *(She turns back to window)* Oh, but why isn't that
shade up? Why aren't they letting us see anything? It's
so haunting . . . Just shadows . . . lights and shadows
moving around, behind that yellow shade, like some weird
shadow ballet.

JOHN   *(Sharply, pulling her from the window)*   All right.
Come away. You're high as a kite! I'm worried about you!
      (The bright light suddenly goes out)

ELAINE   *(Turning back to the window)*   What's happened?
. . . The lights have gone out.

JOHN   I don't know. And I don't care. It's their business.

ELAINE   But—but the room is pitch-dark suddenly. And
the shade—the shade's still down . . .

JOHN   *(With more and more impatience)*   So—they've been
there. They've seen everything . . . *(Leading her back to
the sofa)* Look, police procedure is—police procedure.
We'll read about it in the newspapers. Now sit down and
relax. And calm down. Here, drink your chocolate.
      *(He brings her the cup of chocolate and puts it on the
      coffee table)*

ELAINE *(Shaking her head)* I don't want any. I'm too nervous.

JOHN What about? You don't even know him. He's a total stranger.

ELAINE He is not a total stranger. He's a human being—and my responsibility . . .

JOHN Your responsibility?
(Sirens are heard)

ELAINE *(Getting up, moving to the window)* Oh, they can't be leaving already.

JOHN Why is he your responsibility?

ELAINE John, how can you expect me to not care for some pitiful aging man who looked at me with such a terrible expression in his eyes? As if somebody had betrayed him. Someone did. I know they did.
(Her voice shakes with emotion)

JOHN *(Turning)* All right, I'm getting Blanche up!
(He exits)

ELAINE *(Following him to the doorway)* John . . . don't leave me . . . alone.
(She stands there desperately—then turns back to the window. APPLEBY is seen in the hallway. He tiptoes toward her, cap in hand)

APPLEBY Hello there. (ELAINE *is startled, stares at him. He is a rather odd-looking older man, wearing an oversized sweater, a long wool muffler, and bedroom slippers. He smiles ingratiatingly)* Your back door was open. So I took the liberty. I'm Curtis Appleby—from next door.

ELAINE *(Startled, staring)* Pardon? Who?

APPLEBY *(Glibly)* Appleby, Appleby. The house on your right. I also publish a small weekly newspaper, the *Kips Bay Tatler*, which I *hope* you read . . . I couldn't resist popping in for a few moments . . . I hear that you're the one who saw the dead man, Mrs. Wheeler.

ELAINE *(Uneasily)* How did you know that?

APPLEBY *(Smiling)* From your maid—naturally. The Fräulein. We speak German together . . . My, you've done wonders with this place.
      (He moves gloatingly across the room)

ELAINE Thank you—

APPLEBY I've been so eager to meet you people. You're the Cantwell heiress, aren't you?

ELAINE Yes—
      (JOHN enters, stopping at the sight of APPLEBY)

APPLEBY Ah, good *morning*, Mr. Wheeler. Appleby here —the house with the wall. You're in stocks and bonds. I've seen you running off so many mornings with your attaché case.

JOHN *(Aloofly)* Yes, I've spotted you . . .

APPLEBY *(Smiling)* Although, you know, I keep having the feeling that I've met you in some other capacity . . .

JOHN Don't think so—

APPLEBY Miami Beach in 1962? Las Vegas? The Sands? You didn't ever happen to work as a cruise director on the S.S. *Caronia?*
(JOHN *frowns at him*)

ELAINE *(Quickly, with a nervous smile)* My husband has sold *sail*boats . . .

JOHN Yes. I've been around the sea *all* my life—

APPLEBY There! I almost hit it on the nose, didn't I? The sea. That salty look. A ship was *somewhere* in the picture . . . *(He whips out a pad and pencil, turns to* ELAINE*)* But tell me about your dead man . . .

JOHN What's this?

ELAINE Mr. Appleby's a writer, dear.

APPLEBY The *Kips Bay Tatler.* A local bit of journalese.

ELAINE *(Glancing at* JOHN, *nervously)* Please, we don't want any publicity—

APPLEBY Oh, I'll be circumspect, never fear.

ELAINE We're interested in what the police find. You were in our garden just now. Did you hear anything or see anything?

APPLEBY *(Glancing at her a second)* No, madam. Nothing definitive. *(He walks toward the window)* I face the school, which is horrid enough—with all those unruly young men. *(At window)* But you have a ringside seat, I must say. Did you know I'd put a bid on it last fall?

JOHN On what?

APPLEBY On this house of yours. I tried to purchase it for a friend of mine—the actor Boyd Herrick. *(Slight pause. A strange look flickers over his face for an instant. He smiles)* But you outbid us by a mile, sir. Money talked. Touché.

JOHN *(Moving out)* Excuse me. I'll se what's keeping her —she said she'd be down in a second. *(He exits, calling)* Blanche! BLANCHE!

APPLEBY *(Smiling)* I do hope I'm not interrupting anything? Do tell me what you saw—just off the record eh? In that evil old monstrosity?
   (He pockets his pad and pencil)

ELAINE *(Staring at him)* Evil? Is it—evil?

APPLEBY *(With relish)* Oh, my dear lady, it's always seemed to me to be the very epitome of sordidness and hidden corruption. Do you believe in the occult, the atmosphere that certain places give off? I do. *(He gazes out the window)* Think of its history. Did you know two people committed suicide there in 1852?

ELAINE   No, I didn't.

APPLEBY   Then it became the abode of sweltering immi-
grants fleeing the pogroms and famines of Europe and
coming here to die by the thousands in the sweatshops of
this greedy city. Then later, until the fire gutted it, the
den of prostitutes, bums, drug addicts—all the tragic people of this world whose reward for living is an unmarked
grave in Potter's Field.

ELAINE   *(Drawing her breath)*   How awful. And now a murder has been committed. Do you mean the evil has never
stopped?

APPLEBY   *(Glancing at her sharply, then a shrug)*   Well,
something of the sort, I suppose. But what a contrast to
look out from this—into the very face of death.
        (ELAINE gazes at him for a second. BLANCHE enters.
        She is an attractive redhead of thirty-five or there-
        abouts, with an excellent figure. She wears a tailored
        dressing gown, ornamented with a showy piece of
        costume jewelry—a sailboat pin. She carries a glass of
        water and a pill)

BLANCHE   Oh, Elaine, John just told me about the dead
man. Isn't that wild? How could I have slept through the
whole thing?

APPLEBY   Ah, I've never seen this young lady about. May
I be introduced?

ELAINE   Blanche, this is Mr. Appleby from next door. My good friend, Mrs. Cooke . . .

APPLEBY   How do you do, my dear.

BLANCHE   Good morning . . . *(To* ELAINE*)* Darling, you look pale and tired. Come on and sit down. I was afraid you'd be upset, so I brought your medication.
(She leads ELAINE *to the sofa)*

ELAINE   Mr. Appleby has just been telling me the wildest things about that building . . .*(She stares for a second at the pin on* BLANCHE*'s dressing gown, then turns toward the window)* . . . that it's evil, haunted . . . drenched with horror.

BLANCHE   *(Crossing to window)*   Really? I know that building has always given me the creeps. But practically the same thing happened to a friend of mine last summer in London. He was living in a hotel, and across the way he kept seeing this beautiful woman lying in bed, stark naked. But she never moved, and the light never went off . . . She was dead, of course, but so gorgeous that it broke his heart to notify the police.

APPLEBY   *(Eying her)*   Indeed . . .

BLANCHE   *(Sitting beside* ELAINE*)*   Take your pill.

APPLEBY   Well, I must be running along. *(Studying* BLANCHE*)* But you remind me so much of an actress friend of mine—from Budapest. Stunning woman. But you're from the Middle West, are you not, Mrs. Cooke?

BLANCHE *(Surprised)* Yes. I am. How did you know?

APPLEBY Instinct. But you're not in the theater.

BLANCHE No. I'm a nurse.

APPLEBY A nurse! *(Slight pause, a smile)* Well, the two professions are not so very far apart at that. *(He moves toward the door)* Stay away from bridges, though. She jumped off one in the end—head first, smack into the Beautiful Blue Danube. Didn't drown, broke her neck. *(He chuckles.* JOHN *appears in the doorway)* Ah, there you are again, my friend. So nice to meet you lovely people. And do come to visit me sometime . . . when there's less in the offing. *(He smiles and waves his hand)* I haven't got a palace, but I do have certain unusual curios from various obscure parts of the globe. *(Exiting, he pauses in the doorway.* ELAINE *again looks at* BLANCHE'*s pin oddly.* BLANCHE *notices her mood)* And good luck, Mrs. Wheeler. Long may you dwell in Camelot.
(He vanishes)

JOHN *(Muttering)* Crazy bastard.

BLANCHE *(A shrug, a smile)* Obviously the neighborhood voyeur. *(ELAINE *rises, moves away from* BLANCHE, *looking upset)* What's wrong, Elaine?

ELAINE   I guess that man depressed me, and I—I— *(She looks at the pin on* BLANCHE *'s dressing gown)* Blanche, where did you get that sailboat pin?

BLANCHE *(A smile; touching the pin)*   Do you like it? Lillian gave it to me for Christmas. She thinks I'm nautical, just because that Spaniard in Majorca tried to give me sailing lessons. Is it too gaudy?

ELAINE   No . . . it's beautiful.
      (She moves toward JOHN*)*

BLANCHE   It's bothering you. Something is.

ELAINE   No, it's all right . . . John, would you call the police again? We should have heard something by now . . .

JOHN   Elaine . . .

ELAINE   Please call them.
      *(*JOHN *exchanges a look with* BLANCHE*)*

BLANCHE *(To* JOHN, *sotto voce)*   She's really not too good. *(She crosses to* ELAINE *and feels her forehead)* Your forehead's just like ice.

JOHN *(Having dialed the police number)*   Lieutenant Walker, please.

BLANCHE *(Sitting down beside* ELAINE, *and fingering the pin)* This pin is upsetting you. What is it?

ELAINE *(Moving away)*   I—I'm over it now. It's just—well
—just like the pin Kay Banning wore in the car that day
—with Carl.

BLANCHE *(Aghast)*   Carl! Oh God, Elaine. I'm so sorry . . .
*(She removes the pin and sticks it into the pocket of
her robe)*

JOHN *(On the phone)*   Well, can I speak to someone else?
It's about that murder on Twenty-ninth Street.
(The doorbell rings)

BLANCHE   I'll go . . .

JOHN *(Slamming down the phone)*   No, I'll get it—they
keep you waiting forever.
(He exits)

BLANCHE *(Sitting down beside* ELAINE*)*   I'm sorry about the
pin, Elaine. Why didn't you get me up? I could have kept
you company, read to you. Then maybe none of this
would have happened.

ELAINE   It still would have happened—to that poor man in
the window. *(Rubbing her forehead)* I shouldn't take
those pills. They make me groggy . . .
*(She rises rather dizzily. The front door opens off-
stage)*

JOHN *(Offstage)*   Yes? Who is it?

WALKER *(Offstage)* Mr. Wheeler? . . . Lieutenant Walker, Homicide.

ELAINE *(Overhearing)* It's the police. *(She moves to a mirror, fusses with her hair)* They scare me. I've never been involved with them before.

BLANCHE *(Moving to her)* Yes, you have.

ELAINE When?
> *(WALKER appears in the hallway. He is a glum, sallow-looking man in his fifties, wearing a hat and overcoat)*

BLANCHE *(Quickly)* Forget it.
> *(WALKER enters)*

WALKER Mrs. Wheeler? Which is Mrs. Wheeler?
> *(He looks from BLANCHE to ELAINE)*

ELAINE *(Advancing nervously)* I'm Mrs. Wheeler. Good morning, Lieutenant. Have you any news for us?
> *(WALKER eyes her for a second, then strides to the window)*

WALKER Is this the window where you saw—what you saw?

ELAINE Yes, that's the window. *(He stares out)* Are there any questions you'd like to ask?
> *(JOHN enters)*

WALKER *(Turning)* Yes, I have a question, ma'am. Do you know anything about the crime rate in this city? The increasing crime rate? The number of murders per week we're getting?

ELAINE *(Puzzled)* N-No . . . but I—
 (HELGA pokes her head in the door. She listens)

WALKER It's slaughter, that's what it is. That's what's happening nowadays—

JOHN Lieutenant—

WALKER *(Turning to him)* Earlier tonight I saw a woman —an elderly woman—in a church basement, with her breasts cut off and her sexual parts mutilated. That's the kind of stuff we're getting—and she's just par for the course.

JOHN Please get to the point, Lieutenant. My wife's been up all night, she's very nervous . . .

WALKER *(Turning briefly to ELAINE)* Yeah, I can see she is. *(He turns to JOHN)* Usually I can spot these phone calls, and handle them right off—nervous ladies like your wife. But tonight I missed. *You* made the call. These ladies, they phone the bureau and tell us they've shot their husbands or some neighbor has hung himself—but, well, there isn't one out of a hundred—

ELAINE *(Agitated)* Excuse me, Lieutenant—are you telling us there wasn't anything in that building?

WALKER *(Turning, almost lazily)* Sure, there was something, ma'am. Biggest, damnedest wing chair you ever saw—sitting in that empty railroad flat, by itself, by the window, in the dark. But that was it.

ELAINE But Lieutenant—

WALKER No blood. No dead man. No fingerprints. Not a single sign of violence. Dust all over everything.

ELAINE *(Emotionally)* Lieutenant! That's impossible. I saw him. That—that shade went up . . . *(HELGA, now visible near the door, slowly exits, looking back at the scene, from the stairs)* That chair was there. I'd never seen that chair before. He had to have been in it.

WALKER Lady! Two squad cars. Four men. Half an hour of the department's time—and everybody overworked on double shifts—just to look at a green wing chair?

ELAINE *(Desperately)* There was a body in it.

WALKER All I know is that old lady in the basement—that's a dead body. Good night, ma'am.
(He exits)

ELAINE *(Following)* I saw him. He was bleeding.

JOHN Ellie—

ELAINE John! He's *wrong!*

JOHN *(Softly—sadly)* Okay. What more can we do?

ELAINE *(Desperately)* Please. Please believe me. I screamed. I tore those draperies. *(She walks to the window. Her voice has thickened slightly)* He was right there, in that window—

JOHN *(Moving to her)* Sure . . . Sure . . . Right there. *(He steadies her)*

ELAINE *(Swaying; her hand over her face)* Oh, I'm so dizzy . . .

BLANCHE It's only the medication. It's all right.

ELAINE *(Moving to* BLANCHE, *piteously)* You've got to believe me. *(Her voice keeps thickening)* That shade went up, and—and there he was . . . *(Her eyes flutter closed. She sways)* . . . sitting in the morning sun.

JOHN The sun?

ELAINE *(Rapidly, with eyes closed)* One-four-one-two-seven . . . One-four-one-two-seven . . .

JOHN *(Moving closer, sharply)* What's that, Ellie?

ELAINE *(Eyes closed)* One-four-one-two-seven . . . California . . . Nineteen sixty-four . . . *(*JOHN *glances quickly at* BLANCHE. *Suddenly,* ELAINE *wheels around, facing* JOHN *and* BLANCHE *tensely)* Somebody's doing something! He was staring at me . . . staring at me, with this awful look in his eyes . . . as though he were trying to tell me something . . . *(She totters, as though about to faint.* JOHN *catches her in his arms. Thickly her voice dying*

away) Something unreal, something—incredible . . .
(She collapses in JOHN*'s arms. He carries her to the*
sofa, lays her down gently, and covers her with the
coverlet)

BLANCHE *(Moving to* ELAINE, *touching her gently)* Shall we close the draperies?

JOHN *(Nodding)* Tight. *(*BLANCHE *moves to the draperies and closes them partway)* Tighter . . . Mrs. Cooke.
*(*BLANCHE *closes them all the way. And then she tiptoes out.* JOHN, *after taking one last look at* ELAINE, *leaves, closing the door of the room softly behind him)*

Scene Two

It is five in the evening, the same day. The set is the same library. However, the entire room has been rotated to the right about forty-five degrees—so that the window is now seen at an angle from the audience. Although the draperies are still drawn, when they are opened, we shall be able to see a portion of the darkened, dilapidated tenement and the window with stained yellow shade down, where ELAINE *swore she saw the dead man.*

In the dusk, ELAINE *is lying on the sofa, still dressed in her long robe, underneath the coverlet. The clock begins to strike the hour of five, preceded by Westminster chimes.*

On the striking of the hour, HELGA, *wearing a dark uniform, opens the door and enters. She moves to the window, and opens the draperies. Then she moves to* ELAINE.

HELGA *(Softly)*   Madame? (ELAINE *murmurs drowsily, turns over, her face away from* HELGA) Madame. . . ? *(Still* ELAINE *does not respond.* HELGA *stares down at her a second. Then she moves to the fireplace and lights a fire. Then she moves back to the coffee table, picks up a tray.* JOHN *enters quietly. He is wearing a dark business suit.* HELGA *sees him, gives a start)* Oh, Mr. Wheeler. You got back. . . ?

JOHN   How's she been doing?

HELGA   Up and down all day. On the phone to that police lieutenant. *(Looking at him)* It's a bad city, Mr. Wheeler. It's got nobody you can trust.

JOHN *(Impatiently)*   Okay, okay.

HELGA *(Moving toward the door)*   She hasn't eaten nothing. I made some very nice pudding and—

JOHN   That'll be all, thanks. You can take the evening off.

HELGA   Off?

JOHN   We're dining out tonight. *(Staring at him oddly, she leaves. He moves softly to* ELAINE. *He studies her a second, then he touches her shoulder gently)* Ellie, Ellie— wake up.
    (She wakes with a start. She sits up)

ELAINE   Oh! When did you get home?

JOHN   Just now. Why aren't you dressed?

ELAINE   Oh, I've been in sort of a daze . . . trailing about the house. That medicine!
    (Smiling vaguely, she puts her hand to her forehead)

JOHN   Been on the phone, too. Right? *(She does not answer)* Look, you heard what the lieutenant said. And there's nothing—absolutely nothing—we can do about it.

ELAINE *(Rather guiltily)*   Well, I'm not satisfied with his attitude. *(He turns away impatiently)* I'm not one of his

crazy women who imagine they've shot their husbands—
or some neighbor has hanged himself. They found that
wing chair, didn't they?

JOHN   All right. A wing chair . . . Now, look, it's after five.
Why don't you get dressed?

ELAINE   *(A sigh; sitting on the sofa)*   I've been waiting all
day to talk to you about it. All the lieutenant does is keep
repeating the same old thing, over and over and over.

JOHN   *(Coming over to her, propelling her toward the door)*
Okay, okay. Get some clothes on, and we'll go into it—
from stem to stern. *(Slight pause)* Go along, Ellie . . . I've
got a lot of other things I want to discuss with you.

ELAINE   Like what?

JOHN   Ellie, do what I tell you—please. We've got a big
night ahead of us. Aren't we supposed to be taking
Blanche out for some kind of farewell celebration?

ELAINE   Oh, that's right. I almost forgot. *(She moves out
into the hall)* Did you make the reservation?

JOHN   I will. Eight-thirty okay?

ELAINE   *(A smile)*   Fine.
        *(She leaves. JOHN gazes after her thoughtfully. Then
        he moves to the drapes and closes them. He closes the
        door. Taking a small piece of paper from his pocket,
        he goes to the phone, puts the paper down and dials)*

JOHN *(A low voice)* Hello. John Wheeler speaking. (HELGA *enters)* Hold on a minute. Well?

HELGA Mr. Appleby is here.
(She carries an ice bucket to the bar)

JOHN *(Waving her off)* We aren't seeing anyone.

HELGA He's for Madame.

JOHN She's dressing, and I said we aren't seeing *anyone.*

HELGA *(Departing)* All right, all right, I heard you, Mr. Wheeler.
(She exits. JOHN *closes the door)*

JOHN *(On the phone)* Sorry . . . It's okay, set up for this evening. Don't worry about that. I'm taking care of it . . . Fine . . . When? . . . You have the directions? . . . Very good. Well, thanks . . . Yes . . . Yes . . . Yes . . . Oh, definitely. I will. Right . . . Right. Thank you. *(He hangs up.* HELGA *enters as he is crumpling paper by the fireplace)* I thought I told you to take the evening off.

HELGA *(Closing the door)* Yah, I know, Mr. Wheeler. But I'd like to speak to you a minute, please . . . *(Slight pause)* I can't speak now with Madame. She is too upset. It's not good what's happening. Things, they are not right. *(Looking at him)* I don't like it, Mr. Wheeler. It upsets me very much.

JOHN *(Quietly, looking at her)* What is it, Helga?

HELGA *(Flatly)* I need money. Five hundred dollars.

JOHN Oh? For what—if I may ask?

HELGA *(A tight little smile)* It's my business. But I'll tell you . . . My mother, she is still living in Germany, Mr. Wheeler. And she's very old, she's very sick. I would like to go back there. Pretty soon.

JOHN *(At the bar, fixing himself a drink)* You would?

HELGA So . . . it costs money. Madame, she's very generous. But I don't want to add to her troubles—now. But you, Mr. Wheeler, you're the boss, okay? *(A slight pause.* JOHN *studies her)* I give you plenty of notice. And I don't tell Madame—nothing.

JOHN *(After a slight pause)* Five hundred dollars, Helga? I'll think about it.

HELGA Yah. You think about it, Mr. Wheeler. *(The door opens)* Here's Madame. (ELAINE *enters, smiling, radiant, in evening dress, her hair combed and arranged)* Ach, so beautiful you are.

ELAINE Thank you, Helga. Did Mr. Wheeler give you the evening off?

HELGA Yah. *Danke.*
(She exits)

ELAINE Well, how do I look?

JOHN   Wonderful. Very nice. Something new?

ELAINE   No. I wore it Monday when we took Blanche to the opera.

JOHN   Oh. Well, it looks great on you. *(Fixing himself a drink)* Martini?

ELAINE   *(Crossing to the fireplace)*   Gin doesn't really mix with tranquilizers . . . I love this room in winter, don't you, John? . . . I will have a sherry . . . *(JOHN fixes the sherry. She sits on the arm of the sofa)* It's nice to have this moment alone, isn't it? I adore Blanche, but honestly . . . do you realize we haven't had one cocktail hour all to ourselves in weeks? *(JOHN brings her a glass of sherry)* John, do you remember that big fur rug we used to lie on in Arizona? *(He smiles, touches his glass with hers)* What were all those other things you wanted to talk to me about?

JOHN   Oh, well, I don't want to upset you now . . .

ELAINE   *(Smiling)*   Who's upset? *(Indicating the window)* That was the only thing upsetting me.

JOHN   *(Sitting down beside her)*   Elaine, I took a big step forward today.

ELAINE   Oh?

JOHN   Look, honey, this afternoon I took it upon myself to call up Mount Sinai Hospital, and I spoke to their chief of psychiatry about you.

ELAINE *(Her expression changing)* Oh. And what did you tell him about me?

JOHN I told him all about these bad nights you've been having . . . that you've been plagued with this insomnia most of your life. *(Slight pause)* I also asked him about that clinic in Switzerland. He recommended it—went overboard. He says that it has some of the best doctors in Europe, the accommodations are great, it has a wonderful climate, it's not too far from Geneva . . .

ELAINE *(Shakily)* Geneva is dull.

JOHN *(Rising, walking away)* All right. If you're not interested, forget it. But he did think you needed some kind of help.

ELAINE *(Getting up)* Well, I don't need psychiatry!

JOHN I'm giving you his opinion.

ELAINE I had enough psychiatry eight years ago, and it just mixed me up. Darling, don't you see, if I went to a psychiatrist right now, it would mean I doubted my own mind—I doubted that I saw that dead man. And I know I saw him. It would mean I was losing control, backsliding. And that's never going to happen again. Never. Ever.

JOHN All right, all right, don't get hysterical. Then I'll just tell her not to come.

ELAINE *Her?*

JOHN A woman psychiatrist they recommended at Mount
Sinai. She'd consented to come see you here. I knew you'd
never go to her. *(Slight pause)* And I must say it took a
hell of a lot of persuasion.

ELAINE Here? When?

JOHN Tonight, around six—

ELAINE Oh, John! You *have* been taking giant steps!
(The front door slams)

BLANCHE *(Offstage; caroling)* Helloo . . . It's only me.

ELAINE *(Sotto voce)* Does Blanche know about this?

JOHN Blanche? Do you think I discuss our business with
Blanche?
*(BLANCHE enters, in a chic winter coat and fur hat,
ruddy with cold and carrying packages—plus a wig
box and a small bouquet wrapped in tissue paper)*

BLANCHE Hello! Oh darling, you're up? How pretty you
look. Mmm, my very favorite dress. I felt so guilty about
leaving you today, but Helga was standing guard like a
dragon, and I had a million last-minute things to do
. . . *(Proffering the bouquet)* These are for you. A little
get-well present.

ELAINE *(Smiling)* How sweet. But you didn't have to . . .

BLANCHE I'm afraid I couldn't afford more than half a
dozen at these New York prices.

ELAINE *(Unwrapping the bouquet)* Freesias . . . *(A strange look)* Ch-charming . . .

BLANCHE *(Lightly)* Aren't they delicate?—like little babies' toes. *(She notices* ELAINE*'s expression)* Now what did I do?

ELAINE *(Trying to smile)* N-nothing. They're exquisite. Helga! *(She takes the flowers, moves to the door)* H-how was your luncheon date? *(Turning)* I'll just tell Helga to put them in water. *(Calling)* Helga . . . Would you come up a minute, please?
    *(*BLANCHE *and* JOHN *exchange glances)*

BLANCHE *(Flatly)* My luncheon date was fine. *(To* JOHN*)* What did I say?
    *(*JOHN *shrugs)*

JOHN Pick up your plane ticket?

BLANCHE *(Looking at him)* Yes. I did everything.

JOHN Want a drink?

BLANCHE *(Taking off her coat)* Please.
    *(*HELGA *appears)*

HELGA *(Entering)* Yes, madame?

ELAINE *(Giving her the flowers)* Would you mind putting these into a vase, Helga?

HELGA *(Picking up the flowers, with a slight sniff)* Which vase?

44

ELAINE   I don't know. Maybe a small low bowl. And would you arrange them? Put them in the—the front room, on the Pembroke table, please.

BLANCHE *(Singing it)*   Good *evening,* Helga.

HELGA *(Looking at her coldly)*   Ach, I didn't see you, Mrs. Cooke. How did you get in? I didn't hear no bell ring.

BLANCHE   I have my own key.

HELGA   Ach, she has her own key!
      (With a short, bitter laugh, she exits)

JOHN *(Furiously)*   Ellie, that does it!

ELAINE *(Quickly)*   I'm terribly sorry, Blanche. I can't imagine what's gotten into her. She's so peculiar lately.

BLANCHE   Think nothing of it, dear. I'm used to it. All servants are jealous of nurses. Didn't you know that?

ELAINE   But you're our friend . . . a guest. And on your last night too! Why must you leave us? *(She sighs, moves pensively to* JOHN, *touching him)* Isn't there some way John and I could change your mind? New York seems just the place for you. With all those lovely clothes how can you possibly settle for that remote hospital?

BLANCHE *(A faint smile)*   Oh, the Mayo brothers would adore to hear their clinic called remote.

ELAINE   I just meant it seems so far away . . .

BLANCHE   Nothing's far away with jets, darling. No, I'm looking forward to it immensely. It's time I got the feel of a real hospital again—and real people—after pushing all those rich bitches around in their wheelchairs on the Rome-to-Riviera circuit.

ELAINE   But Minnesota in the wintertime! *(A pause)* Why don't you just stay here and marry Larry? He sounds perfect for you. Wait until his divorce is final?

BLANCHE *(After a slight pause)*   Darling, you don't know Larry. Getting married again is the last thing on his mind . . . No, that's over. *Terminé.* It served its purpose. *(Jumping up suddenly, she moves to her packages, picking up the wig box)* But let me show you what I bought today. You'll never guess. A brand-new me—for my new life.
    (She starts unzipping the wig box)

ELAINE   Not a wig? But, Blanche, your own hair is so lovely . . .

BLANCHE   I'm bored with being a redhead. You know what they say about blondes. *(She removes a long blond wig, from the wig box. It is set on a white styrofoam wig block with a face.* ELAINE *stares at it)* Isn't it divine? It's a Super-Scandinavian.

ELAINE *(Recoiling)*   Oh . . .

BLANCHE *(Waving the wig about)*   What's wrong with it? Too silly?

ELAINE *(Leaving the vicinity of the wig and* BLANCHE*)* No, it's charming. It really is.

BLANCHE *(Following with the wig)* Elaine, you hate it. What is wrong?

ELAINE *(Nervously, uneasily)* Nothing. Try it on. I guess I just don't like wigs on wig blocks. *(Turning away)* Go ahead, Blanche. It's beautiful. And I shouldn't be so hypersensitive. Otherwise, God knows, I will need that psychiatrist.

BLANCHE *(Moving toward her, still holding the wig)* What psychiatrist?

ELAINE *(Evading her—and the sight of the wig)* Some woman John's hired to talk me out of that dead man.

JOHN Elaine, that's not the reason.

BLANCHE What's her name?

JOHN Dr. Lake. Tracey Lake.

BLANCHE Tracey Lake?

JOHN You've heard of her?

BLANCHE Of course. She's an authority on insomnia. Why, she wrote a book that's practically a classic, though I can't remember the name, on the neuropathology of sleep patterns. We used it in nursing school. Elaine, how lucky.

ELAINE *(Faintly)* Please . . .

BLANCHE *(Moving to* ELAINE, *the wig in her hand)* Darling, what's the trouble?

ELAINE *(Hysterically)* I can't stand to look at it. Put it away! *(She knocks the wig block out of* BLANCHE*'s hand)* Get rid of it!

JOHN Elaine! What the hell's the matter with you?

ELAINE I'm sorry . . . *(She sinks into a chair)* Blanche—I apologize. It just looked exactly like her head.

BLANCHE Whose head?

ELAINE Hers. Kay Banning's.

BLANCHE Oh, God. I'm sorry . . .
(She puts the wig block back into its box)

ELAINE It's all right. You never saw her.
*(*HELGA *enters)*

HELGA Mr. Appleby, madame.
*(*APPLEBY *glides in swiftly. He is dressed in a double-breasted suit of a rather old-fashioned cut—with a flower in his buttonhole)*

APPLEBY *Good* evening, one and all. Pray pardon the intrusion. *(Gliding toward* ELAINE*)* I came to inquire about our good lady's health. Fully recovered, Mrs. Wheeler? What a charming *robe de style*. A little token I whipped up.
(He offers her a small bottle)

ELAINE   For me? Thank you.

APPLEBY   Frightfully good for whatever ails you. A Trappist monk gave me the recipe. I practically live on it. I'm here to offer you my services, as well.

JOHN   Your services?

APPLEBY   *(A slight bow)*   Murder is my hobby—and after this morning, how could I resist?
(He glides to the window)

JOHN   Now, just a minute—

APPLEBY *(Avoiding his eye)*   The Case of the Vanishing Corpse, eh? Now one sees it—presto, it's gone! *(He snaps his fingers, smiles)* A classic in fiction—indeed even commonplace, with certain authors. But where did this one vanish to? *(To* BLANCHE*)* What do *you* think—ducky?

BLANCHE *(Staring at him narrowly, gathering up her packages)*   I don't think.

APPLEBY *(Raising his eyebrows, a smile)*   You don't *think? Everybody* thinks. Even houseguests are allowed to—think . . . occasionally . . . *(*BLANCHE *exits)* And I can hear those busy little wheels whirring—

JOHN   Now, look here, Appleby—

APPLEBY *(Turning, fingering a chess piece)*   Beautiful chess set. Renaissance? Florentine? *(He glides to the window)* Yes, where on earth did he go—that sullen, silver-haired stranger?

JOHN   Do give us your opinion.

APPLEBY   Down a trap door? Up a chimney? *(BLANCHE enters)* Or was he possibly just chopped up? Marinated —in lime? Stuffed under a floorboard, crammed into a coalbin? . . .

HELGA *(Under her breath)*   Gott, dot's terrible . . . *(Crossing herself, she leaves hastily)*

APPLEBY *(Turning to ELAINE, with a gleaming smile)*   Or was he real—at all?

ELAINE *(Staring at him)*   Oh, yes, Mr. Appleby. He was. He *was!*

APPLEBY   I meant—not human. A waxwork, possibly? A hoax? A dummy . . . A grisly *arranged* spectacle?

JOHN   Ridiculous.

ELAINE   Oh, no. No. I never even *thought* of such a thing. Of course not. Who would dream of doing it?

JOHN   Exactly.

APPLEBY *(Darkly)*   The rich attract enemies. *(Turning suddenly on JOHN—as ELAINE looks out the window)* What's *your* opinion—friend?

JOHN (Glowering)   My opinion? I think you don't belong here.

APPLEBY   Eh? Good heavens. Well! I thought we were good friends. *Neighbors.* Well! *Good* night. I am due at

a cocktail party. Frightful bores, aren't they? *(He glances at* JOHN *and* BLANCHE, *then at* ELAINE*)* Cocktail parties. *(Whisking out)* Keep me apprised though. I'm *fascinated.* At any hour of the day—or night.
(He exits)

JOHN   That son-of-a-bitch . . .

BLANCHE   I hate that man. He's sadistic . . .

ELAINE   But you don't suppose—

JOHN *(Turning on her)*   Elaine, whatever he told you, put it right out of your head.

ELAINE   But it might explain something . . .

JOHN   Explain what?

ELAINE   The disappearance . . . the shade going up and down . . . *(She moves to the phone)* I think I'll call the lieutenant about it.

JOHN *(Moving quickly, trying to block her)*   Now, don't be insane—

ELAINE   But it was just, in some ways, like a peep show—a hideous peep show. Put on for my benefit. And I did only see him for a minute or two. John—really. Mr. Appleby might have hit on something.
(She again moves to the phone. Again JOHN *blocks her)*

JOHN   The man's a fool! He's a phoney.

ELAINE *(Moving past him)*   Then, isn't that all the more reason we should talk to the lieutenant?

JOHN   Oh, Elaine—

ELAINE   Well, he did want to buy this house, didn't he?
(She reaches for the phone)

JOHN *(Raising his voice firmly)*   Elaine, I don't want you to call him!

ELAINE *(Staring at him)*   Why not . . . darling?

JOHN *(More strongly)*   You've called that poor bastard enough today. You're just humiliating yourself—

ELAINE   Why are you so fierce about it?
(He looks at her)

JOHN *(Bitterly)*   Okay. Go right ahead. *(He strides toward the door)* Make a fool of yourself—but leave me out of it!
(He exits, slamming the library door. A brief silence. She turns to BLANCHE *and then begins to dial 9–1–1)*

ELAINE   Oh, he's never yelled at me before. And over such a silly little thing. *(On the phone)* Hello, I'd like to speak to Lieutenant Walker, please. It's Mrs. Wheeler again. *(Her voice is shaky. The door opens cautiously. As she talks,* HELGA *is seen standing outside with the bowl of freesias. She listens, unseen by* ELAINE*)* Lieutenant

Walker? Elaine Wheeler speaking. I'm terribly sorry to disturb you again, but do you suppose that dead man could have been a hoax? Deliberately placed there? Some sort of grisly arranged spectacle, to scare me out of my wits—to make us leave this house?

BLANCHE *(Sotto voce to* HELGA*)*   I thought she told you to put them in the front room?
    *(*HELGA *glares at* BLANCHE. *She listens to* ELAINE*)*

ELAINE   Well, possibly, but not necessarily a dead body . . . though I was perfectly sure it looked like one. *(*HELGA, *holding the flowers, creeps further into the room)* The blood certainly looked real . . . I beg your pardon? Enemies? Well, I don't know of any. Though it's true we own some valuable things . . . *(*HELGA *puts the flowers on the library table with a small thud. She glares at* BLANCHE *and exits)* No, nothing's ever been touched . . . You will look into it, Lieutenant?

BLANCHE *(Moving to* ELAINE *and laying her hand on her shoulder)*   Elaine . . .

ELAINE   Well, thank you very much. I—really—
    (She hangs up)

BLANCHE   He hung up on you?

ELAINE *(Walking away, dispiritedly)*   No. He seemed fairly interested.

BLANCHE *(Moving after her)* Darling, you have no enemies. You've always been so sweet and generous and good. No, I think what John was trying to say is that your only enemy is yourself—your nerves, your insomnia . . .

ELAINE Blanche, that man had nothing to do with my nerves or my insomnia!

BLANCHE All right. All *right!* If you're not careful, you're going to work yourself up just as you did in California.

ELAINE *(Frowning, staring at her)* What does that mean?

BLANCHE *(Rather awkwardly)* I mean you were very sick then, and it strikes me that you're beginning to suffer from the same depression symptoms.

ELAINE Depression symptoms! Blanche, really!

BLANCHE Elaine, I recognize the signs. There's the same old excitability, the inability to sleep, the same fixation on something unimportant.

ELAINE Unimportant? Do you call murder unimportant? And then being told there wasn't any murder? What kind of talk is that?

BLANCHE *(Looking at her)* *Was* it murder—or a hallucination?

ELAINE *(Staring at her)* Hallucination? I've never had hallucinations.

BLANCHE *(Shaking her head)*   Darling, don't you remember California and all those times when you thought you saw Carl standing at the foot of your bed, standing there with his head all bashed in?

ELAINE *(Walking away)*   I was always having those nightmares.

BLANCHE *(Following her)*   Those were not nightmares. You were wide-awake and screaming that Carl was really there. Just as you screamed that—that man was there this morning.
(ELAINE stares at her. There is a second's silence)

ELAINE *(In a choked voice)*   Are you trying to tell me that man was just a hallucination?

BLANCHE   Yes, a kind of quick hallucination that's called an eidetic image . . .

ELAINE   A—what image?
(As she stands there, staring at BLANCHE, with her back to the window, we see a faint light flicker on in the second-story window behind the shade and dance out. Neither BLANCHE nor ELAINE sees it)

BLANCHE   An eidetic image. It springs from the subconscious, from some deep trauma or anxiety . . .
(Again the light goes on and off)

ELAINE *(Pacing)*   Blanche, you're wrong. He couldn't have been. He wasn't. He wasn't Carl. Carl was young and slender and blond. This man was heavy—

JOHN *(Entering)* She's only trying to help you . . . *(Suddenly the light in the window glows on, and* BLANCHE *sees it. She stares at it)*

ELAINE Well, she's not. Eidetic images. Depression symptoms. You know I've stopped thinking about Carl. Now, why rake up that mess. . . ? *(Suddenly she notices the light in the window. She moves to the window)* Look. What's that?

    *(*JOHN, BLANCHE *and* ELAINE *all stare at the lighted window)*

JOHN Probably just kids. The place is open territory . . . *(A man's shadow crosses the shade)*

ELAINE That isn't any child.

JOHN All right. Probably a cop. You've been calling them all day . . .

ELAINE *(Rather darkly)* No. Someone's in my building.

JOHN *Your* building?

ELAINE I'm beginning to feel it's mine. John, please call the lieutenant. *(Moving to the phone)* Never mind, I'll call—

JOHN *(Striding to the desk)* No, I'll do it . . .
    (He dials 9–1–1. During the following scene, the light in the window keeps going on and off. The shadow of the empty wing chair is projected on the shade

*momentarily perhaps, and the man's shadow appears
and reappears)*

ELAINE *(Returning to the window, addressing* BLANCHE*)*
That's no eidetic image! It's real. I told you something
very sinister is going on over there.

JOHN *(On the phone)* Lieutenant Walker, please. John
Wheeler. If he speaks to me, he's got to be a saint
. . . Oh, good evening, Lieutenant. This is Wheeler, John
Wheeler. I want to apologize, Lieutenant, for giving you
one hell of a day . . .

ELAINE Oh, please, John—just tell him.

JOHN But this time we think we have something. It's a
light—in that Twenty-ninth Street building—and we've
seen what appears to be a man's shadow moving around.
Is it one of your men?
(A slight pause. ELAINE *moves tensely toward* JOHN*)*

ELAINE What's he saying? What's he telling you?

JOHN He's checking it out . . . *(Into the phone)* Oh, I see.
Well, thanks, Lieutenant, she's been upset. *(He hangs up,
rises from the desk and moves to the window)* He has no
men stationed there. But they're sending a squad car.
They'll take care of it.
(He closes the draperies)

ELAINE John, what are you doing? Please. I want to see.

JOHN *(Blocking her way to the draperies)* Dr. Lake is due any minute now.

ELAINE Dr. Lake? You didn't phone her? But I thought we'd cleared that up. Please, both of you—*(*BLANCHE *walks toward the door)* You saw those lights in there. And now the police are coming. It's real, John, real. Don't shut it out.

JOHN It's probably some drunken prowler. Ellie, I'm much more worried about *you. (*BLANCHE *tiptoes out. He draws Elaine from the window)* I want you to feel better, and you know you're never going to—until you face up to the real thing that's causing all this trouble.
(We hear faint sirens approaching)

ELAINE *(A small voice; looking at him)* What—real thing?

JOHN *(A quiet smile)* Carl. *(She stares at him, then turns her back)* You've never gotten over him.

ELAINE That isn't true. It isn't.
(She starts looking for a cigarette)

JOHN Ellie. Even when I met you, two years after it happened, you were still all churned up about Carl. Why, that first night—out there on the beach. We were crazy about each other—wild. Then you called me by his name. And later you burst out crying. Remember? *(She finds a cigarette, a matchbook. He takes the cigarette from her)* Carl was that dead man, wasn't he?

ELAINE   No. Please, please. I—I've gotten over him.
(She stares down at the matchbook, reacts strangely)

JOHN *(Shaking his head sadly)*   Ellie, you don't get over things that easily. And I'm telling you, Carl's just gone underground . . . like those swampy rivers in Florida. You don't even know they're there. Then one day suddenly they suck you in.

ELAINE   No, no, no, no . . . NO! *(With a cry, she walks to the window. She sweeps open the draperies)* Somebody is doing something. *(The window in the tenement across the way is dark. Her gaze returns to the matchbook in her hand. She bows her head)* Oh, God . . . God help me.

JOHN   Ellie. Stop it!

ELAINE *(Handing him the matchbook)*   Just look at this matchbook. Somebody wrote those numbers down.

JOHN *(Taking the matchbook)*   What? What numbers?

ELAINE   There.

JOHN   One-four-one-two-seven. So?

ELAINE   Carl's license number. I thought nobody in the world knew those numbers except me.

JOHN   Well, *I* don't. I can't even remember my own license number. Probably somebody's phone number.
(He tosses the matchbook into the fire)

ELAINE Somebody's *phone* number!

JOHN Ellie, you can't go all to pieces over every god-damned little thing!

ELAINE Little thing? That wig was not a little thing. That dead man or that shadow over there. You saw that shadow and that matchbook. *(Moving to him desperately)* John, why can't you believe me? Why are you deserting me?

JOHN I'm not deserting you.

ELAINE *(Clinging to him)* I—I admit I'm on the edge. I'm frightened—scared to death. But I need you. And I love you. Say you love me.

JOHN Of course, I love you—
        (He takes her in his arms. They embrace. BLANCHE enters. They move apart)

BLANCHE *(Quietly)* Excuse me. Doctor Lake is here.

ELAINE *(Detaching herself, tensely)* I didn't hear the bell.

BLANCHE I saw her car pull up to the curb, so I let her in. Wasn't that all right?

DR. LAKE *(Entering)* Good evening.
        (DR. LAKE is a middle-aged woman, dressed in a hat and coat)

BLANCHE Dr. Lake, this is Mrs. Wheeler. And Mr. Wheeler.

DR. LAKE *(Coming forward, extending her hand)* How do you do? What a charming home you have.

ELAINE *(Eying her with a nervous smile)* Thank you. I'm afraid it isn't very charming at the moment . . .

JOHN *(Quickly)* So good of you to come, Doctor. *(Ushering her toward the front drawing-room)* Would you like to use this room in here? It's more private . . .

DR. LAKE Anywhere you say, Mr. Wheeler. *(As they move out into the hall)* What a pretty sitting room. So feminine. Coming, Mrs. Wheeler?

ELAINE *(Tensely, indecisively)* Blanche—do I have to do this?

BLANCHE *(Patting her)* Good luck, Elaine . . .

JOHN *(Reappearing)* Let's go, Ellie. *(He takes* ELAINE*'s arm and leads her through the door.* DR. LAKE *lingers in the hall)* Oh, by the way, Doctor, I meant to ask you. Do you know anything about the Rilke Clinic in Switzerland?

DR. LAKE The Rilke Clinic? For insomniacs? Yes, indeed. An excellent place.
(She exits with ELAINE*)*

JOHN Well, thank you. That's what they said at Mount Sinai.
*(*JOHN *reenters from the hall)*

BLANCHE *(Looking at him)* I think you need another drink.

JOHN *(Advancing toward her, grimly)* I thought at lunch today you agreed to leave.

BLANCHE Yes?

JOHN So, what's with all this sleight of hand—freesias, wigs. . . ?

BLANCHE I don't know, John, I swear—

JOHN Look, Blanche, I don't want things stirred up around here. Not now.

BLANCHE Who's stirring things up? You got the psychiatrist. *(Slight pause)* And by the way, how did you get *the* Dr. Lake to make a house call on such short notice?
(The doorbell rings)

JOHN By calling her. Money talks.

BLANCHE *(Thoughtfully)* I thought she'd be a lot older.

JOHN You mean you think she's *not* Dr. Lake?
(There is sudden commotion from offstage—trampling feet, door slamming, and HELGA*'s shrill voice)*

HELGA *(Offstage)* Yah? Hey, wait a minute. Stop that!

HOKE *(Offstage)* I wanna speak to her. *(*HOKE *appears in the doorway. He is a large shabby man, middle-aged, with iron-gray hair and a very wrathful expression. He carries a flashlight. He has a Bronx accent)* Where's Mrs. Wheeler? *(To* BLANCHE*)* You Mrs. Wheeler?

BLANCHE   No. God! Who are you?

JOHN   What in hell is this?

HELGA *(Entering)*   He's that delicatessen man. He pushed the door open.

HOKE (*Whirling to her, then to* JOHN)   Damn right I am. Sam Hoke, a respectable citizen. I'm suin' you people, see? What the hell kinda people are you? Sickin' the cops on me—

JOHN   Sicking what cops?

HOKE   I had a right to go into that building, see? I live next door to it. I own a store next door to it. You hear a murder's been committed, you don't sit around on your ass all day—

JOHN   Hey, hey, hey, hey! *(A slight smile)* You mean you were the man in the building with the flashlight?

HOKE   Yeah, yeah . . .

JOHN   I see. Well, sorry. Our mistake.
(He tries to usher HOKE *out)*

HOKE   Some mistake! Every time that wife of yours calls the cops and them squad cars come screamin' down the street, whaddya think that does to my business? It ruins it, that's what. It scares off the customers. They think another murder's been committed—and already I got robbed twice. So what happens to my property value? What happens to my potato salad, what happens to my chicken salad, not to mention my roast beef—which happens to be two seventy-nine a pound wholesale?

HELGA   What happens to it?

HOKE   Into the garbage pail!

JOHN   *(Propelling him toward the door)*   Okay, okay. I'll make it up to you.
   (The door opens. ELAINE *enters)*

ELAINE   What's going on? Who's here?

JOHN   Nothing. Nobody. I'll tell you about it later.
   *(*HOKE *turns and stares at* ELAINE *from the hall across the room)*

BLANCHE   *(To* ELAINE*)*   It's all *right*, darling.
   *(*DR. LAKE *appears, looking at the scene curiously)*

ELAINE   *(Staring at* HOKE*)*   All *right?* *(A sharp intake of breath, a step forward; low and intense)* John, call the police. This is incredible! Who's doing this? Who is?

JOHN   *(Grabbing her by the arm)*   Doing *what*, for God's sake?

ELAINE   My God, don't you know who this is, John? It's the dead man! *(As* JOHN, HELGA, BLANCHE, DR. LAKE *and* HOKE *stare at her, she says shakily, but with conviction)* The same eyes, the same hair, the same face!

HOKE   Lady, I never saw you before in my life!

ELAINE   I saw you in that window . . . I know that it was you!

JOHN   Ellie!

ELAINE *(Strongly, vehemently)*   Yes, John! Yes! YES! *YES!*
(As they stare at her, the curtain falls)

Curtain

ACT TWO

SCENE ONE

Twenty minutes later. The curtain rises on the same set in the same position as it was at the end of Act One. Only ELAINE *and* DR. LAKE *are onstage.* ELAINE *is pacing back and forth. The door to the hall is closed. The window draperies are still open.*

DR. LAKE *(Turning her head to* ELAINE*)* If we could proceed, Mrs. Wheeler, it might help the situation . . .

ELAINE *(Getting up)* Doctor, he *was* that dead man. Believe me. *I* saw him. *I'm* the one to know.

DR. LAKE *(A pleasant smile)* Yes, but we've gone into it—

ELAINE Please. Just listen for a moment more. Nobody wants to listen. Nobody takes this case seriously. Nobody in the world believes that anything strange is going on— but it is, it is. I know it is. Somebody's doing something —using that old tenement . . .

DR. LAKE *(Slight pause—walking to the window)* Why? For what purpose?

ELAINE I don't know. *(She runs her hand through her hair)* I don't know why that man would come here. What he hoped to gain, why he lied to everyone . . .

69

DR. LAKE   Hmm. Well, let's hope it will work out—ulti-
mately . . . *(Leaving the window; an awkward smile)* Mr.
Hoke—was that his name?—did look so extraordinarily
alive I personally found it impossible to imagine him as
dead, or seated in any pose, in any chair whatsoever.

ELAINE   Oh, when people want something they can do
almost anything . . .
        (She shivers)

DR. LAKE   Are you cold? Would you like a sweater? Or
perhaps this to slip around you? *(She picks up the coverlet,
wraps it around* ELAINE, *glancing out the window. We
hear the sound of wind)* Such bitter weather. Vermont
weather. *I* come from Vermont . . . the great mountains
. . . the deep snow . . . *(Leading* ELAINE *to the sofa)* Where
were you born?

ELAINE   In San Mateo.
        (She continues to pace)

DR. LAKE   California? My dear husband was a Californian.
(Looking at ELAINE*)* Interesting. You seem more East
Coast.

ELAINE   My father had a ranch there . . . but other houses,
other places. We traveled a good deal.

DR. LAKE   Did you? Is he still alive?
        *(*ELAINE *shakes her head)*

ELAINE *(After a pause)* I was nineteen when he died. He left me—without any warning.
(She gets up restlessly, searches for a cigarette)

DR. LAKE *(Eying her—softly)* And your mother?

ELAINE He never remarried. *(Picking up the cigarette)* Oh . . . my mother? She died when I was born. All he had was *me*.

DR. LAKE *(Touching Elaine's arm as she reaches for a match)* Please. I'm sure you enjoy them, but it tends to distract you. *(She turns to the window briefly)* And I lost someone very dear recently, an inveterate cigar smoker. It's my private aversion, sad to say. *(*ELAINE *puts down the cigarette)* How were you all he had?

ELAINE Who?

DR. LAKE Your father, dear.

ELAINE Oh . . . Well, I was an only child unfortunately, and overly protected, I'm afraid. When I was three, he gave me my first Shetland pony. And when I was five he took me to Europe for the first time. Nothing was too much for Daddy's fertile imagination . . . *(Smiling, reminiscently, she rises, walking to the window, with the coverlet around her)* At my debut, just imagine, he—he even lined our entire driveway with all of his prize cattle— Black Angus heifers—and every one of those gorgeous beasts had a crown of flowers on her head. There were torches in between. It was like Versailles . . . and I danced till dawn—that lovely long-lost night . . .

DR. LAKE   Did you suffer from insomnia as a child?

ELAINE *(At the window, reminiscently)*   Yes, I was one of those children who couldn't even manage to take a nap. They tried to make me. There was this little Catholic school next door to our house in Paris. In the afternoons, I'd lie awake for hours listening to the children singing "Frère Jacques" and imagining the most impossible stories in which I was always the heroine . . .
   (A slight pause)

DR. LAKE   When did this present attack begin?

ELAINE   I don't have attacks. I just have difficulty sleeping. My father couldn't sleep. But *he* owned oil companies, railroads . . .

DR. LAKE   Nothing special was disturbing you?

ELAINE *(Removing the coverlet, laying it aside)*   No, nothing. Absolutely nothing . . .

DR. LAKE   There'd been no change in any of your personal relationships?

ELAINE   None whatsoever.

DR. LAKE   Things were going smoothly between you and your husband?

ELAINE *(Staring at her)* Yes. Just fine—until that horrible thing happened.
(She nods toward the window)

DR. LAKE How long have you been married?

ELAINE Six years.

DR. LAKE It's been a good relationship?

ELAINE Of course. *(Slight pause)* We've had our ups and downs. We're very different temperamentally. But I believe in marriage, Doctor . . . the ebb and flow . . . giving and sharing. Couples should adjust to each other, not fly off at the first rainstorm.

DR. LAKE *(With enthusiasm)* Oh, so do I. Yes, that's so true of *any* intimate relationship. *(Slight pause—cautiously)* And that young lady who opened the door? Blanche, is it? She lives here?

ELAINE Not exactly.

DR. LAKE What position does she occupy?

ELAINE Position? Blanche Cooke? Why, she's my very best friend. She's just been visiting us—on her way to the Mayo Clinic. *(Frowning)* Why would you bring her up? She's so loyal and devoted. She's been so good to me in so many ways. She practically saved my life . . .

DR. LAKE Saved your life?

ELAINE   Yes, after my first husband died.
(She seems to catch herself. For a second she looks as though she wants to bite off her tongue)

DR. LAKE   Your husband? . . . Oh, then you've been married before.

ELAINE *(Moving quickly to her)*   Excuse me, Doctor. What are eidetic images? Do they exist?

DR. LAKE   What happened to your first husband?
(We see the doorknob of the door leading to the hall turning. The door opens just a crack)

ELAINE   He—died—and I don't want to talk about it. It doesn't have a thing to do with my insomnia . . .

DR. LAKE   Why?
(The door closes suddenly)

ELAINE *(Jumping up)*   What's that?

DR. LAKE   Nothing. I heard nothing. What happened to him?

ELAINE   But I *did* . . .
(She starts walking toward the door)

DR. LAKE *(Interposing)*   Perhaps it was the wind. *(She tries to lead* ELAINE *back to the sofa)* Please, what happened to him, dear?

ELAINE   I know it wasn't the wind. That window can't be opened. Somebody's outside—

DR. LAKE Let's see. *(Walking to the door, she opens it, looks out into the hallway)* No one. Just the clock. *(She closes the door)* These old houses are so draughty. *(She takes* ELAINE's *hand and leads her back to the sofa)* No one is listening . . . Mrs. Wheeler, I'm a doctor. And I've learned to keep a secret. It's mandatory in my profession. And I can assure you there are none I've ever betrayed.

ELAINE *(As though the word had struck her)* Betrayed . . . *(Looking at her)* Are you sure you want to hear this? It's so—ghastly, so—

DR. LAKE *(A smile)* Ghastliness is what I hear all day. *(She sits down, still holding* ELAINE's *hand. Reluctantly, nervously,* ELAINE *sits down)* Come, now. Your hand is so cold . . . Who was he? When did all this happen?

ELAINE *(Hesitantly at first, then with growing emotion)* It was eight years ago . . . H-his name was C-Carl. He was a very brilliant young lawyer who was going into politics . . .

DR. LAKE *(Softly)* Go on . . .

ELAINE I loved him. I looked up to him. After Daddy died he seemed—like heaven—all over again . . .

DR. LAKE Yes?

ELAINE *(Shakily, but trying to tell it calmly)* We'd been married about two years. We lived in Beverly Hills. And I was—finally expecting a child . . . the only child I've ever been able to conceive. *(Slight pause)* And then . . . Could I *please* have a cigarette?

DR. LAKE   Yes.
(Offering her the pack)

ELAINE *(Taking the cigarette)*   Thank you. And then one day—one bright day in February . . . *(She tries to light the cigarette; it takes a couple of matches. We hear the wind rattling the panes)* February twelfth, 1964. *(Puffing on the cigarette, she suddenly stares at the window, rises)* That shade? It didn't move. . . ?

DR. LAKE   No, child . . . What happened?

ELAINE *(After another glance out the window)*   I had just been to the hairdresser's. I was driving back through Coldwater Canyon, listening to the car radio, when suddenly I—I rounded this downhill curve, and saw this wrecked car on the road . . . people starting to run to it. It looked familiar somehow—the car. A black convertible, with someone at the wheel. And then I saw the license plates. One-four-one-two-seven. The top was down. It was hanging over the side of the mountain . . . where there were m-masses of s-small white flowers . . . freesias . . .
(She turns her gaze for a moment to the freesias in their bowl)

DR. LAKE   Your first husband was at the wheel?
(ELAINE nods. She cannot speak for a moment. She

gazes at the freesias, then she turns, her voice more choked and tight)

ELAINE   With his h-head all bloody—and his eyes s-staring . . . *(DR. LAKE shakes her head sympathetically)* I—I managed to reach his side. But then . . . I saw the girl. She was lying on the seat beside him, with her neck broken—but still smiling at me. This twenty-year-old blonde from across the street. Kay Banning was her name . . . And her skirt was up above her thighs . . . His hand was still inside her dress . . .

(She turns away, trembling, silent. The wind keeps rising)

DR. LAKE   *(Sensing there is still more)*   Yes?

ELAINE   *(Turning with a ghastly look, but still forcing herself to speak)*   It had been going on for months . . . I lost my baby. And then . . . I didn't want to live. I swallowed twenty sleeping pills. But that's a long time ago, except—

DR. LAKE   Except what?

ELAINE   *(Bursting out)*   He betrayed me! That's the thing I'll never get over. *(She sinks down, her hands over her face)* N-never. . . !

(She sobs convulsively)

DR. LAKE   *(Her hand on ELAINE's shoulder)*   Oh, my dear, my dear . . . *(Patting her)* Yes . . . Betrayal, as you choose to call it, is extremely painful—*(Turning, with a vague sad*

77

smile)—even to the strongest of us. It diminishes us so
. . . *(A slight pause.* DR. LAKE *rises)* I would like to speak
to you further about this. Would you be willing to come
to my office sometime?

ELAINE *(Rising)* Yes . . . I might. I think I'd like to . . .

DR. LAKE *(Touching her shoulder, a smile)* Good. Then I'll
arrange it with your husband. *(She starts walking out, then
pauses, fishes in her purse)* Meanwhile, please try this
medication. Two at bedtime.
(Handing ELAINE *a small bottle, her eyes suddenly fix
on the window and she starts)*

ELAINE What's the matter?

DR. LAKE *(A quick smile)* Nothing. *(She moves to the
window, then glances back at the lamps)* Just a reflection.
(She goes to the window) You might try closing those
curtains at night. It *might* prove beneficial. *(Moving to
the door)* Good night, Mrs. Wheeler.

ELAINE Good night, Doctor.

DR. LAKE Sleep well.
(She exits. ELAINE *stands looking after her. Again we
hear the wind. She shivers. She glances toward the
window nervously, then takes a step toward the doorway and calls)*

ELAINE John? *(No answer. The clock begins to strike the
first Westminster chime of the hour. She takes another
step toward the door)* Blanche? Helga? *(Her voice is*

choked. The chimes continue. The clock begins to strike the hour of seven. She gazes around the room and at the window, as though panicky. Then, as though impelled to look out, she moves to the drawn draperies and tentatively peers out. Suddenly she utters a bloodcurdling scream and sinks slowly to the floor) No . . . oh, no . . . OH, NO!
(She moans. BLANCHE *rushes in)*

BLANCHE   Elaine, what is it? What happened? *(*ELAINE *stares at her. She looks toward the window. Then she looks at* BLANCHE. *Her expression is vacant)* What's wrong?
(She shakes ELAINE. ELAINE*'s expression does not change.* DR. LAKE *enters. She moves to* BLANCHE *and* ELAINE*)*

DR. LAKE   What happened?

BLANCHE   I don't know . . . I was upstairs.

DR. LAKE   *(Hand on* ELAINE*)*   Mrs. Wheeler? *(*ELAINE*'s stony expression does not change)* Mrs. Wheeler, what is wrong?
*(*JOHN *enters)*

JOHN   *(To* BLANCHE*)*   What's going on here?

DR. LAKE   She seems to be in shock.
*(*JOHN *kneels beside* ELAINE. *He takes her in his arms)*

JOHN   Ellie—what is it, Ellie?
*(*ELAINE *stares down at his hand. She gives a strange shaky little laugh. Then her lips begin to quiver. She lays her head on his shoulder)*

ELAINE *(Brokenly, half inaudibly)* It was . . . a woman . . .

JOHN A woman?

ELAINE In—in that other window. Dead. A blond woman lying in that other window . . . l-like a limp rag
doll . . .
(She bows her head)

JOHN Ellie, there couldn't have been anything. Nothing.

ELAINE *(Bursting out, rising)* Call the lieutenant, please.
Won't somebody call him? *(She tries to run to the door.*
JOHN *restrains her)* Let me go over there!

DR. LAKE We'd better get her up to bed.
*(*JOHN *picks* ELAINE *up in his arms. She struggles)*

ELAINE *(Hysterically)* No. Do something. Call him.
Please, John—let me go!

JOHN *(Carrying* ELAINE *out)* Sure, sure. Don't worry. I'll
take care of everything.

ELAINE *(Offstage, incoherently)* Young . . . so pretty
. . . please, please . . . help . . .
*(*BLANCHE *and* DR. LAKE *exit.* ELAINE*'s voice dies. A*
second's silence. Then HELGA *appears, looking up the*
staircase darkly. She creeps into the room. She goes
to the window and looks out. Then she turns to the
library table, seeing the doctor's bag lying there. She

opens it and looks inside. BLANCHE *is seen coming down the stairs, and quickly* HELGA *closes the bag, puts it down, fiddles hastily with an ashtray and exits, staring hard at* BLANCHE *as she enters.* BLANCHE *closes the door after* HELGA *softly. The room now has a shadowy, gloomy, rather eerie atmosphere. She then moves to the phone and dials one digit)*

BLANCHE *(A low voice)* Operator, I'd like to send a telegram. Can you connect me with Western Union, please? *(Slight pause. She toys with the freesias still in their bowl on the library table)* Western Union? I'd like to send a telegram and charge it to this number. Murray Hill three-six-oh-nine-eight. To Rochester, Minnesota. The Mayo Brothers Clinic. Nurses Registry. The message reads as follows: "Unavoidably detained due to serious illness in the family." *(*JOHN *enters quietly. She does not see him at first)* May have to cancel job. Regret inconvenience. *(She notices* JOHN. *She smiles faintly)* Sign it Blanche A. Cooke. Will you read that back to me, please? *(*JOHN *slides his arm around her waist. He moves his body close to her)* Thank you.

JOHN *(Embracing her)* You just couldn't wait, could you?

BLANCHE *(Nestling against him)* John, I couldn't very well leave now . . . *(Suddenly we hear a cry from offstage and* ELAINE*'s agonized voice)* John! *JOHN!*
(He lets BLANCHE *go and moves to the door)*

BLANCHE *(Following)* John . . . *(Smiling, touching him)* You know, what you need is a nice long vacation, in the sun . . .

> *(He looks at her. They kiss passionately. Then he lets her go and exits. She stands there, looking after him, faintly smiling. Then she picks up the pill bottle and the doctor's bag from the library table, walks to the window, peeps out through the curtains and then exits, closing the door)*

Scene Two

It is three days later at night. The Westminster clock is striking the hour of nine.

Again the stage has been rotated to the right, so that the window now occupies center stage. The draperies are closed.

As the clock is striking, ELAINE *enters. She is dressed for traveling and carries a mink coat over her arm, a hat and purse.*

She sets down the coat, hat and purse and moves to the window. She opens the draperies.

As they open, we are given a full opportunity to see, front on, the tenement opposite, and what all the characters in the drama have previously been able to see—the two windows almost directly on a level with ELAINE*'s window. Both windows have yellowing ragged shades, drawn to the sill. There is also the suggestion of upper and lower floors burned and charred by fire, with here and there some windows broken. Yet the scene has a strange haunting beauty. It is lit by moonlight.*

ELAINE *stands looking out for a second. Then she moves to the telephone. She picks up the receiver and dials 9–1–1.*

ELAINE *(Softly, urgently)* May I speak with Lieutenant Walker, please? It's Mrs. Wheeler . . . He's not? You're sure he isn't? . . . Well, if he happens to be there, will you tell him, please, that I'll only take a minute of his time?

(JOHN appears in the doorway, carrying a couple of expensive suitcases. He listens) I'm just anxious to know if there's anything new on those two murdered people in that building on Twenty-ninth Street . . . There's not? Well, when he does come in, will you ask him to call me anyway? *(JOHN exits)* I'm leaving the country tonight and may be gone for quite a while, but I'd love to check with him just one more time. I'll be here for the next half hour. Thank you. Thank you so much.

(JOHN enters, carrying an attaché case. She hangs up)

JOHN *(Putting his attaché case on the library table)*   Come on, Elaine. It's been so nice and calm for the last three days. Don't start again.

ELAINE *(Walking to the window)*   But I just can't believe all that murky pap about eidetic images and anxiety states. That woman was nothing like *Carl's* girl friend.

JOHN   What did you say?

ELAINE   I said she wasn't anything like Carl's girl friend, Kay Banning. She was much prettier . . . and older. I can see the poor thing still. And she wasn't smiling at me. She looked shocked. She had this ghastly look of surprise—

JOHN   Okay. Got your passport and travelers checks?

Elaine *(Still at the window)*   Yes. They're in my purse.

JOHN *(After looking in her purse, moving to the attaché case)*   Fine. Look, there's one more thing I'd like you to do. *(Taking papers from the attaché case)* I'm sorry to bring it up this late, but those damn lawyers are so slow. . .

ELAINE *(Uneasily)* What lawyers?

JOHN *(Placing the papers before her)* Our tax lawyers. They felt and I felt that since you were going away, it might be wise for you to sign this . . . *(Giving her a pen)* Here, Ellie. There—where it says "Spouse."

ELAINE But, John, our return isn't due for months, is it? Really! Surely I'll be coming back long before income-tax time.

JOHN Of course. I certainly hope so. But who knows how long it's going to take? You're going over there for a rest and to get well . . . *(As she lingers)* Come on. Just sign it, get it over with. It took a lot of trouble to prepare. Why won't you take my word for it?
    (HELGA appears in the doorway)

ELAINE All right. Should I read any of this?
    (She riffles through the pages)

JOHN If you're that interested, of course.

ELAINE It looks endless. All these funny names—like alphabet soup. What does MAXCO mean? And DIPTICO? I've never heard of them.

JOHN Not DIPTICO, dear. DIPCO. D-I-P-C-O. It's a big real-estate firm of ours, and MAXCO's a steel outfit.

85

HELGA   May I speak to you a moment, madame?

JOHN   Later. We're busy.

HELGA   Madame?

ELAINE   I'll be with you in a moment, Helga.

HELGA   *Danke.*
       (Sourly, she withdraws)

JOHN   *(Moving to the attaché case, bringing out another form)*   And now the estimate . . .
       (He gives it to ELAINE*)*

ELAINE   The estimate? Oh, dear, it seems so awfully final.
       *(*BLANCHE *enters)*

BLANCHE   Elaine, darling, excuse me, but could I ask you a favor? I'm having so much trouble packing, so could I leave a few of my things here and send for them later, when I'm settled in Des Moines? Is that all right with you?

ELAINE   Of course. And as far as I'm concerned, I don't see why you felt you had to go to Lillian's. You're welcome to stay right here.

BLANCHE   Oh, that's sweet of you, but it wouldn't look right.
       (Over ELAINE*'s head, she exchanges a smile with* JOHN*)*

ELAINE *(Handing* JOHN *the signed forms.* JOHN *puts them back into his case)* I've been such a nuisance. I've upset so many of your plans.

BLANCHE Darling, do you think I'd have gone off and left you when you needed me? I can get another job anywhere. Trained nurses are in great demand. And besides, Lillian's agog to have me. And I'm sort of curious myself, to see what's happened in Des Moines—who's gotten married, who's died . . .

ELAINE *(Rising and going to the window)* Well, you're still welcome to stay right here . . . *(Looking out)* Oh, Mr. Appleby's in our garden. John, Mr. Appleby's outside!

JOHN What?

ELAINE *(Waving, calling, rapping on the windowpane)* Mr. Appleby! Mr. Appleby!

JOHN *(Moving to her)* Elaine, have some sense. How did he get through that gate? Elaine, now what in hell . . . ? *(To* BLANCHE*)* Check that back door.
*(*BLANCHE *exits)*

ELAINE But he was looking up at me smiling, and pointing to those windows. Maybe he's heard something.

JOHN What? There's nothing for him to hear.

ELAINE There might be.

JOHN   He's an idiot. Ellie, use your head. You know he just upsets you. Why do you even bother with a nut like that? We've got a plane to catch.
(APPLEBY enters)

APPLEBY   Mrs. Wheeler. You beckoned me? *(To JOHN)* Good evening, friend. *(To ELAINE)* I heard about the second body. A curvaceous blonde? How delectable. They're being slaughtered by leaps and bounds. Oh, have you seen the piece I wrote?

JOHN   *(Sullenly)*   What piece?

APPLEBY   *(Whipping out a small newspaper)*   The *Kips Bay Tatler.* Nothing questionable. Just a small vignette of your beautiful home. Your antiques. *(To JOHN)* Your sailing trophies. I hope you'll put it on our house tour some day. I'm on the committee. The money goes to slum beautification. But you're leaving us, I heard. For Switzerland, of all places.

JOHN   *(Picking up his attaché case)*   Yes. The plane leaves at eleven.

APPLEBY   Really? A rather odd time. Well, I shan't stay— more than a second. But Switzerland! That's such a milk-chocolate country. A skiing weekend? Business perhaps?

ELAINE   No. Mr. Wheeler isn't going.

APPLEBY   Isn't he? But of course. Business calls. How has the market been doing lately?

JOHN   Elaine, the limousine is due in ten minutes.
(He exits)

APPLEBY   *(After a brief pause)*   You know, he really hasn't
one iota of gaiety.

ELAINE   We've all been under a strain.

APPLEBY   Oh, of course. I've been absolutely at sea myself.
(Walking to the window) Two murders in less than
twenty-four hours. Now, that's a peck of grue to have to
swallow, isn't it? I just don't know what to think—how
to explain the entire phenomenon.

ELAINE   You don't believe it could have been a hoax, Mr.
Appleby?

APPLEBY   Eh?

ELAINE   A grisly arranged spectacle?

APPLEBY   Madam. That might have done for one, not two.
In the same day? No, *two* dummies strike me as a trifle
—excessive.

ELAINE   Then what do you think could have happened?
*(APPLEBY looks at her a second. Then he lowers his
voice)*

APPLEBY   Have you ever considered, Mrs. Wheeler, that it
might have been, as they say in the vernacular—an inside
job?
*(ELAINE stares at him a second, then she shakes her
head and walks away)*

ELAINE   No, I'm sorry, Mr. Appleby. Oh, no. Oh, certainly not. I'm positive that no one in this house could possibly have been involved.

APPLEBY *(Moving to* ELAINE*)*   Very well, I didn't mean to disturb you. It's just that I'm sincerely interested. And so sorry that you're leaving. This is such an exquisite haven. I shall miss my visits here, brief though they have been. *(She turns and smiles at him faintly)*

ELAINE   Well, thank you, Mr. Appleby.

APPLEBY   And I'll miss you too, of course, with your great doomed eyes, your haunting look . . . Do you know, from the moment I first saw you standing at that window in your long white gown, or pacing up and down, like some fragile ghost, you intrigued me. You seemed like a jewel in some pastiche setting, an emerald in a cardboard box.

ELAINE *(A nervous smile)*   Oh, Mr. Appleby, I'm not that interesting.

APPLEBY   Oh, but you are. And that's why I've intruded. When one has time on one's hands . . . is lonely, getting on in years . . . *(Slight pause; his voice shows a tinge of emotion)* Well, to tell you the truth, my best friend, my boon companion of twenty years, recently left me for a wealthier—and younger individual.

ELAINE   Oh, I'm sorry.

APPLEBY *(Rather brusquely)* No matter, no matter. One can't do a thing about these situations—ever. *(He moves to her and takes her hand)* Goodbye, lovely lady. My love to the Matterhorn. And luck be with you. *(He smiles, looks into her eyes)* Somehow I feel it will be—in this crystal ball of mine.

ELAINE *(Moved)* Mr. Appleby—*(She gestures toward the room)* Would this be of any help?

APPLEBY What, madam?

ELAINE *(Moving toward the library table)* This house. My husband will be leaving shortly. It will be empty for at least a month. *(She opens a drawer of the library table, and takes out a key)* And if you'd like to use it—

APPLEBY *(Flabbergasted)* Mrs. Wheeler!

ELAINE *(Offering him the key)* I'd be delighted if you would.

APPLEBY My dear.

ELAINE *(Smiling, giving him the key)* You might even look for clues if you still believe in your theory.

APPLEBY *(Pocketing the key)* Oh, delicious! *(Taking her hand)* Thank you. I shall be honored to be the caretaker of Camelot.

ELAINE *(Smiling)* Goodbye, Mr. Appleby.

APPLEBY   Goodbye.
(*He moves to the door.* JOHN *enters with two suit-cases*)

JOHN   Let's get going, Elaine.

APPLEBY   Just leaving, Mr. Wheeler-Dealer.

JOHN   What? What's that you called me?

APPLEBY   Mr. Wheeler-Dealer. Oh, where's your sense of humor, Captain? It just tripped off my tongue.

JOHN (*Advancing on* ELAINE)   What's this guy been telling you?

APPLEBY (*Airily*)   Fairy tales.
(*He exits*)

ELAINE   Are those Blanche's suitcases?

JOHN   Yes. She's riding with us in the limousine. Then I'm dropping her off at La Guardia. That okay with you?

ELAINE   Of course.
(*The doorbell rings*)

JOHN   Now, who the hell is *that*?

ELAINE   Probably Helga's cab. I should say goodbye to her.

HELGA (*Offstage*)   Yah, come in, please. (*Calling*) Mr. Wheeler! Look who's here. Lieutenant WALKER!
(WALKER *strides in. He is followed by* VANELLI. WALKER *looks as glum as ever*)

ELAINE *(Breathlessly)* Lieutenant Walker, you got my message? You have news for me?

*(*HELGA *appears, hovering in the background)*

WALKER *(Turning, eying* ELAINE *sourly)* No, I wouldn't say I had news for you. I'm here on behalf of your neighbors.

ELAINE My *neighbors?* What neighbors?

WALKER The neighborhood. I'm here to ask you to please lay off. Stop stirring up trouble. Stop ringing my phone all day and all night. Because as far as I'm concerned, and as far as the police department is concerned, we've marked our investigation "Closed." Right, Vanelli?

VANELLI *(Humbly)* Right, sir. Right.

(He starts looking at the paintings surreptitiously)

ELAINE You can't mean that, Lieutenant. How can the case be closed? It was only Tuesday that I saw those two people. How can you just dismiss it all in three days?

WALKER Well, I'm sorry, ma'am. We did our best.

ELAINE You couldn't have. You couldn't have gone into it very *deeply* . . .

WALKER That filthy joint has been thoroughly searched from top to bottom, believe you me. There never was one shred of evidence. None. Vanelli can tell you—

VANELLI Lady, the dust was like a carpet—wall to wall. The rats were running all around.

ELAINE *(Sinking down)* I still can't believe it. I can't believe it. *(Desperately, rising)* Are you sure you've gotten all the facts, the information? How about that man I identified—that Mr. Hoke?

WALKER Who?

ELAINE A big man in his fifties. My husband must have called you about him. He calls himself Sam Hoke. But he's the image of that man I saw in the window.

VANELLI If you mean Sam Hoke who owns a delicatessen store, why, I've known him since I was a kid. I used to live here in this neighborhood. *(A slight chuckle)* He makes the lousiest potato salad in New York City. But he's just gone to Florida.

ELAINE Florida?

VANELLI Yeah, his wife died down in Florida. He'd sent her there for the winter.
(ELAINE sinks down, visibly shaken)

WALKER You've got to realize what these calls do to people. We've got so much real crime in this city, they're scared out of their wits as it is. Just suppose, for example, you were a little old lady, living all alone in a railroad flat, across the street from that vacant building. Or a family with kids. It would scare the hell out of you just to hear those sirens—hear some rumor that a murder, *two* murders had taken place there. Why, you've got women so nervous, ma'am, they won't walk past that building. Kids talking about the bogey man. That's not right, ma'am. It's not fair. This city's lousy enough. And when people are poor, they're stuck with it. They haven't any place else to go.

(JOHN *enters*)

ELAINE *(Faintly)* I still believe I saw those two people.

WALKER Okay, Mrs. Wheeler, go on believing it. But don't call us any more.

JOHN Mrs. Wheeler's leaving tonight for Switzerland.

WALKER *(Brightening visibly)* Switzerland? She *is?* Well, why didn't you tell me? That's a very nice country. Very low crime rate. *(Moving to the door)* Then that about wraps it up.

JOHN *(Shaking his hand)* We appreciate your trouble. Thank you, Lieutenant. *(He moves to the door)* Ellie, all the bags are down. I'll just get my coat.

(He exits)

WALKER *(Looking back at* ELAINE, *who is seated with her hands over her face)* Cheer up, ma'am. You're not the first one or the last this has happened to. And there's one thing you did accomplish.

(He moves to the window)

ELAINE *(Emptily)* What?

WALKER   Well, we had so many complaints and phone calls from the neighbors that we finally got in touch with the real estate agents and made them board up those lower windows. See?

ELAINE *(Looking out)*   Oh. I—I hadn't noticed . . .

VANELLI *(Grinning)*   No way to get in there now, without a key.

ELAINE *(Ruefully)*   That's—small comfort, I'm afraid.

HELGA *(Piping up)*   Who owns that building?

WALKER *(Taking a piece of paper from his pocket)*   It's owned by something called the DIPCO Corporation.

HELGA *(Reacting)*   DIPCO!

WALKER *(Moving to the door, addressing* ELAINE*)*   Yeah. Big real estate combine.

VANELLI   Like I told you before . . .

WALKER   Bought it for some client of theirs. But they sure let it go to pot. Goodbye, ma'am.

ELAINE *(On the verge of tears)*   Good night, Lieutenant.

VANELLI *(Nodding cheerfully to a painting)*   Great Matisse!
        *(*WALKER *and* VANELLI *exit, leaving* HELGA *and*
        ELAINE *alone)*

HELGA   Poor Madame. Please don't feel bad, madame. You got a minute?

ELAINE *(Raising her head, emptily)* Yes, Helga. You're leaving?

HELGA Shh . . . *(She puts her finger to her lips, walks to the door, softly closes it and returns)* I should maybe have spoken to the police just now. But it's not my place maybe. *(Her voice becomes low and conspiratorial)* Did you hear what the police lieutenant said about that building?

ELAINE Unfortunately—every word, Helga.

HELGA *(Approaching her)* Owners! DIPCO, madame. Does that name mean anything to you?

ELAINE What?

HELGA *(Gesturing toward the window)* I couldn't help overhearing, madame, when you were signing those papers. DIPCO, your company, it owns that building.

ELAINE *(Blinking)* Oh, that's right. I must speak to Mr. Wheeler about it.

HELGA *(Aghast)* Mr. Wheeler? *Gott in Himmel!* You should phone that information to the police lieutenant.

ELAINE The police lieutenant? *(A short strange little laugh)* Oh, he's stopped listening to me. The Case is Closed . . . and that's not the real question anyway, Helga.

HELGA Question? What question? Madame, what's happening to you? It's been too much for you, a shock?

ELAINE *(Vaguely, dreamily, moving to the window)*   The question is . . . the question is . . . What really happened that awful morning?

HELGA   Why, you saw that shade go up! You saw that dead man, yah.

ELAINE *(Brooding, staring at the window)*   I thought I did. But did I? Did I, Helga? Did that shade go up—or was it only me?

HELGA   Madame! Of course you did. You told me you did. You screamed. You ripped the drapes. Look. Here . . .
         (She shows ELAINE *the torn draperies)*

ELAINE *(Shaking her head sadly)*   I don't know any more . . . *(Cocking her head to one side)* Did it go up at all? That's what I'm asking myself. Or did I somehow *make* it go up?

HELGA   Make it? Madame? What for?

ELAINE *(Walking away, broodingly)*   And all those other things . . . that matchbook and that delicatessen man. Were they a part of it, too? Were they just innocent things I used—for—some monstrous purpose?

HELGA *(Desperately)*   Madame, I don't know half what you are talking about. But you *did* see it go up. You called the police. Please, don't give up now. Don't throw away your life.

ELAINE *(A sad smile)*   My life? My life's worth nothing if this is what I did. I need help badly. I need to go to Switzerland. *(A distant cab horn honks)* Oh, there's your cab. Don't worry about me. It's a long way out to Staten Island.

(She moves to her purse, picks it up, and opens it)

HELGA *(A sigh)*   Yah, a long way . . . *Gott!* I don't know what to do. You're sure you'll be all right? You're not in danger maybe?

ELAINE *(A sad smile)*   Danger? What could possibly happen?

HELGA *(Twisting a button on her coat)*   So . . . Well, I didn't mean to upset you. I guess I don't know everything. *(Moving toward the door)* Goodbye, madame.

ELAINE   Wait a minute, Helga. *(She takes some money from her purse)* I think this will be enough for you to go and visit your mother.

(She offers HELGA a clutch of bills)

HELGA *(Overwhelmed)*   Madame! For me, madame? Oh, no, it's too much. You knew about my mother?

ELAINE   Very little escapes me.

HELGA   Oh, *danke, danke.* You are a real princess. *(She is close to tears)* And *danke*, much obliged, madame, for all the nice references. I hope they treat you good over there. A nice plane trip. *Auf Wiedersehen*, madame . . .

ELAINE   *Auf Wiedersehen,* Helga.
(She kisses HELGA. HELGA *exits as* BLANCHE *enters with a glass of water. She stares at* BLANCHE; *one final glance, then leaves)*

BLANCHE   Here's your pill, dear, for the plane ride.

ELAINE *(With melancholy, walking away)*   How sad it sounds in German, doesn't it? *Auf Wiedersehen,* dear house, dear life, dear—everything—
(Her voice chokes in a sob)

BLANCHE   Now, darling, you'll be coming back to it soon. Come on, take your medicine. *(She offers the glass to* ELAINE*)* You know how you hate flying.

ELAINE   There's such a hollow feeling all of a sudden. The house is full of echoes. It seemed like such a lucky house when we bought it. Now suddenly I feel I'll never see it again.

BLANCHE   Did that busybody say something to upset you?

ELAINE *(Shaking her head)*   No. Helga loved me. Do you love me, Blanche?

BLANCHE   Elaine, what a thing to say. Of course I love you. *(She hugs* ELAINE*)* I love you. John loves you. You're well loved. Here. Are you planning to drink this, or shall I flush it down the john?

ELAINE *(Taking the glass)*   No, I'll drink it. *(A slight pause)* Where's the pill?

BLANCHE   Oh, I dissolved it in the water.

ELAINE   Why? You never did that before.

BLANCHE   It was a little flaky—the last one in the bottle. *(ELAINE looks at her a second, then sets the glass down. BLANCHE picks it up) Now* what? *(A slight pause) Drink it. What's* the *prob*-lem?
(Her voice is edged with tension, controlled)

ELAINE   *(Walking away)* I'm so tired of taking pills, Blanche. I've taken so many in my life. And maybe this . . . the last one in the bottle . . . should be the one I didn't take.

BLANCHE   *(Sharply)* All right. That's up to you. *(She picks up* ELAINE's *mink coat)* Ready?

ELAINE   *(Quietly)* Yes . . . There's just one more little thing. Blanche, are you really going to Lillian's tonight?

BLANCHE   *(Staring at her)* Elaine! Of course I am.

ELAINE   She doesn't seem to be expecting you.

BLANCHE   What makes you think—?

ELAINE   I called her about the sailboat pin to find out where she'd bought it.

BLANCHE   You called Lillian about the sailboat pin?

ELAINE   It was such an unusual one. And she said she was leaving today for San Francisco for a visit . . . and she hadn't heard a word from you in months.

BLANCHE   What?

ELAINE *(Walking away)*   Of course, it's none of my business, Blanche. But where are you really going when you leave here tonight?
> *(A second's pause.* BLANCHE *lays down* ELAINE's *coat)*

BLANCHE   It—it is your business, Elaine. And I'm sorry. I've been fibbing about it to you and John. But I thought it might upset you. You've been so sick. I knew it was against your principles.

ELAINE   What principles?

BLANCHE *(Quickly, glibly)*   Oh, it's all that Larry's idea. We—got together again . . . and—well—he's asked me to go on a little trip with him.

ELAINE   Oh, really?

BLANCHE   There! I *knew* you'd disapprove. *Really*, Elaine, these things are nothing. They're taken for granted by *most* people.

ELAINE   Where are you going?

BLANCHE   To Nassau—some place warm . . . *(Slight pause; more heatedly, moving to the window)* Darling, you said yourself I didn't belong in Minnesota! Besides, it's up to *me*, isn't it? And as far as I'm concerned, life is for *living*, not moping around.

ELAINE I—see.

BLANCHE Oh, God. Why did I even tell you? It's such a petty thing to squabble about at the last minute. Darling, I'm sorry. I didn't mean to lie about Lillian. Please don't be *angry* at me.

ELAINE Angry? A lie is such a small betrayal.

BLANCHE And don't use words like "betrayal" either. It's scarcely apropos . . .
    (JOHN strides in, wearing his overcoat)

JOHN The limousine's here.

BLANCHE I'll get my purse.
    (She exits hastily)

JOHN *(Picking up* ELAINE*'s coat)* Let's put on your coat. Elaine!
    (She moves away)

ELAINE You want me to go to Switzerland very badly, don't you, John?

JOHN *(Coming to her with the coat)* Yes. Come on, wrap up.

ELAINE *(Evading him)* It means—a great deal to you that I should get on the plane tonight and leave the country, doesn't it?

JOHN Of course. It means a great deal to me that you should get *cured*. Cured of—

ELAINE *(Interrupting)* Is there any other—thing—that means a great deal to you? *(He turns and stares at her. From now on his manner grows increasingly tense)* Or anybody?

JOHN No. For God's sake. What's the matter with you? Of all the stupid times—

ELAINE John, please, let's be honest—

JOHN No, there isn't. Let's get out of here. *(Again he moves to her with the coat)*

ELAINE *(Rather quaveringly)* Will I ever see you again?

JOHN *(More and more exasperated, tense)* Ellie, what's gotten into you? Stop all this talk. We've got a plane to catch.

ELAINE *(Near tears)* I know. But, John, I have to know the truth. I can't get aboard that plane without . . . without being perfectly sure . . .*(Blurting it out)* John—are you Larry?

JOHN What?

ELAINE Larry. Blanche's boyfriend.

JOHN *(Putting the coat down)* Ellie. For God's sake. What put that idea in your head? *(A short laugh)* Blanche's boyfriend . . . Larry. Was that the name?

ELAINE He's taking her to Nassau . . .

JOHN   Nassau? I thought that she was going to Des Moines. Well, that's a switch. But God, Elaine, do you think I'd bother with a dame like Blanche? With *you* around? I'd be nuts . . . Come on.

ELAINE   *(Faintly, slipping away)* I—just wanted to know . . .

JOHN *(More irately)*   Well, now you *do* know. Let's go!

ELAINE   It—it still seems awfully strange . . .

JOHN *(More angrily)*   Oh, *what's* strange? What in hell is so strange about getting rid of your insomnia, straightening yourself out—*doing* something—for once?

ELAINE   I just meant—

JOHN   Well, what *you* mean and what *I* mean—that's two different things usually. Right? *I* say we're going and you say we're not. I say we have a plane to catch and you want to play Twenty Questions. Well, I'm warning you, Ellie. I've had it.

ELAINE   I—I'm not trying to question you. I never have—

JOHN *(Slight bitter laugh)*   That's a joke.

ELAINE   A—joke . . . ?

JOHN *(Moving toward her slowly, rather menacingly)*   Ellie, you've always been questioning me, not in words, but in your eyes . . . *Watching*—like I was some kind of wild animal, some wildcat you'd tamed.

ELAINE *(Breathlessly)*   That isn't true—I—

JOHN *(With rising anger)*   But this time I'm not taking it
—hear? I'm warning you. I've stuck by you six years. SIX
years. I haven't left. I haven't gone around the *corner!*
But I could hit the road right now . . .

ELAINE   John, don't say that. I love you . . . I just don't want
to do it—say goodbye . . .

JOHN   Well, you've got to. Or something's going to *ex-
plode!* Queers running in and out. Cops coming in and
out. And *you* screaming about *murder.* That's sick. It's
sick as hell, baby!

ELAINE   But I'm *not* sick . . .

JOHN *(Hoarsely)*   *Stop* resisting *everything* I say . . . *Noth-
ing* I do or say ever pleases you! I get you a psychiatrist!
I run my ass off. I listen to that garbage. Why? Why?
Why won't you do what I say?

ELAINE *(Gasping)*   John! John! I will . . .

JOHN *(Pacing, ranting)*   Who wants a wife who doesn't
sleep at night? Who wants a woman who's in love with
her dead *father?* It's enough to drive you crazy. Dead
bodies, sailboat pins, matchbooks! *(He sweeps a box off
the coffee table)* Things that never NEVER were there!

ELAINE *(Very, very quietly)*   But they *were* there.

John *(Jerking violently)* Don't say that. Ever again!
(He takes a menacing step forward)

ELAINE *(Quickly, fishing a key from her pocket)* Then how
do you explain this key? I found it in this house. And it
says DIPCO on it. DIPCO, our company. *(Her voice
begins to choke)* They own that building! They bought it
for some *client!* And this—oh, God—I'm sure—is the
key to that old wreck!
(She walks to the window)

JOHN *(In choked, stifled tones)* Ellie, you can't *do*
this . . .

ELAINE I want an explanation, John. I'm not leaving until
I get one.

JOHN Explain *what?*

ELAINE This key, this *key!* Who uses it? Who owns it?
Who brought it here? *(Brandishing it, choked up)* John,
don't lie—any more.

JOHN This is insane. It's crazy!

ELAINE *(Her voice becomes more frenzied)* Everything's
insane and crazy. Nothing is true or real. It's a sea of lies
—a quicksand—in which I'm sinking, drowning . . .
(BLANCHE enters. Turning on her wildly) Blanche, do you
know anything about this?
(She holds up the key)

BLANCHE *(Looking quickly at* JOHN*)* About what?

ELAINE *(More feverishly)* This key—this *key! (Beginning to pace around the room, runs her hands through her hair)* Oh, I wasn't going to say anything. I promised myself— persuaded myself . . . Because nobody listens . . . nobody cares. . . . I'm the neurotic. I'm the crazy lady . . . but . . . *(Turning to* JOHN *with feverish eyes)* Was it you who posed? Not Mr. Potato Salad?

JOHN *(Frenzied, moving to* ELAINE, *addressing* BLANCHE*)* Turn off those lights and close that door!

BLANCHE *(Sotto voce to him)* Calm down, for God's sake. *(She closes the door, puts out the lights)*

ELAINE *(To* BLANCHE*)* And did *you* run over there later with some sort of blond wig on? You were never in the room when it happened. It isn't far. Just through the back door, in and out the window. *(Half singing, mockingly)* Go in and out the window . . .

BLANCHE *(To* ELAINE*)* Please, darling, just relax!

ELAINE And Carl was such an easy out, wasn't he? Eidetic images. *Dr.* Lake. She didn't even *look* professional. *(She laughs hysterically, paces about)*

JOHN *(More quietly, trying to get to her)* Now listen, Elaine . . .

ELAINE *(Pathetically mad)* But you were all I had, darlings. All, all, all. Darling, darling Daddy, with a crown of flow-

ers on his head. The saviors became the Judases. The evil
never stopped.
(She stares toward the tenement)

JOHN *(Jerking shut the draperies, then advancing on* ELAINE*)*
Now look, Ellie, *nobody's* done anything. The limou-
sine's here. And we'll just quiet down now, go quietly.
That key . . . Give Blanche the key. It might be any key.
(She darts away)

BLANCHE *(Moving in on* ELAINE*)* Yes, darling, I never saw
it. *(She turns off the remaining lamp)* Let's go. Look. All
dark . . .

ELAINE *(Evading them; to* BLANCHE, *brightly, feverishly)*
Oh, what an Angel of Death you are. So bright, so glitter-
ing, with your hand eternally on my shoulder. Standing
there amidst your freesias . . .

BLANCHE *(Sotto voce)* John, she's sick, she really is. I'm
going to call a doctor.
(She moves toward the phone)

ELAINE *(Moving quickly toward the door, holding up the
key)* No. *This* will prove who's right. *(Darkly)* You own
that building, John. And you put that chair there. *(In-
sanely)* And *you* pulled that shade up. Why? Because
you hated me, that's why. Because you wanted *me* in
there.

JOHN *(Moving toward her, frenziedly)* SHUT UP!

ELAINE   Me. Dead. Me. Murdered. Boarded up. No Switzerland. Just a little trip across the garden. Just a perfect airtight crime!
(He lunges for her. ELAINE *runs out the door)*

BLANCHE *(Screaming)*   JOHN!

ELAINE *(From the hall—a wild laugh)*   Come on, John. See if this key fits.
(She disappears, running down the stairs. A door bangs open, bangs shut)

BLANCHE *(Struggling to hold back* JOHN*)*   We didn't do it! We didn't do it! She's crazy. Leave her alone. Let me call an ambulance. Don't go, John! I'm afraid of what you'll do to her! I don't want her hurt!

JOHN *(Frenziedly)*   The hell you don't! You bitch! *(He shoves her aside violently. He rushes off down the stairs, calling hoarsely)* Elaine!

BLANCHE   John! *(She rushes to the window, parting the draperies with her hand, looking out and down, breathing heavily. We cannot see what she sees. She gasps) Oh, my God . . . (She raps on the pane, screaming)* John! JOHN!
(She rushes precipitately to the door and out. We hear her footsteps running down the stairs, pausing, and then the sound of the door creaking open, then creaking shut. Silence a second or two. Then the clock begins to chime the hour of ten with Westminster chimes. The room remains in darkness. Moon-

*light and shadows play eerily over the draperies.
When the clock has finished striking, there is a second of silence, then we hear the honk of an automo-
bile, the sound of a siren in the far distance, and then
silence again. Suddenly it is broken by the sharp yowl
of a cat. It resembles a human scream. There is silence, and then we hear the sound of a shot in the
distance. A dog begins to bark in the distance. There
is another shot and then another in close succession.
Silence. The waiting has by now become almost un-
bearable. A jet begins to approach and pass over the
house. It fades away. Silence. We hear the clock
ticking. And then we hear the sound of a door creaking softly open and creaking shut.* ELAINE *enters the
room. She is icily calm. Her face reveals no trace of
emotion. And then we realize that she is holding a
small revolver. She lifts the revolver, and then sight-
ing along it, removes a bit of tissue from her pocket
and wipes the gun off carefully. Then, holding the
gun with the tissue, she goes to the library table,
opens the drawer and places the gun inside. She
blows her nose with the tissue. She moves to the
phone and dials 9–1–1. She begins to breathe more
heavily)*

ELAINE *(Tensely and breathlessly, as in all the other calls to
the police)* Hello, I'd like to speak to Lieutenant Walker,
please. This is Mrs. Wheeler calling . . . Yes, Mrs. John
Wheeler . . . But it's urgent. Terribly urgent. I have to

talk to him. I must. *(A slight pause)* Lieutenant? This is Mrs. Wheeler. I think there's something you should know . . . Yes, I am. I'm leaving in a few minutes . . . But Lieutenant, there *are* two dead bodies in that building . . . Yes, there are. Murdered. A man and a woman. And they're sitting side by side in there. It's true, Lieutenant. I swear it . . . Yes, I know you've heard it a million times. But this time you've got to believe me. Oh, please. Please send somebody in there to check. *(A long pause. She holds the phone receiver out a slight distance from her head and listens to it with a faintly mocking smile. Then she speaks into the receiver again)* All right. I'm sorry. You absolutely refuse then? . . . And that's your final decision? . . . Very well, Lieutenant. That's exactly what I always thought you'd say—from the very beginning.

(Smiling, she hangs up. She walks to the window and opens the draperies. Nothing is to be seen, except the same view of the tenement—the dilapidated windows, with shades drawn. She stands there looking out for a second, turns and then reaches for her hat. Putting her hat on, and then her mink coat, she begins to sing "Frère Jacques")

Frère Jacques,
Frère Jacques,
Dormez-vous?
Dormez-vous?

(She gazes one more time out the tenement as she flings her mink coat over her shoulders and picks up her purse)

John—are you sleeping?
John—are you sleeping?
Ding—dong—ding . . .
(She exits on the final "ding," closing the door behind her. The stage lighting dims, and very gradually through the walls of the tenement we vaguely discern the interior of a dingy room, with two figures, one in a wing chair, the other sprawled nearby. The light is ghostly, eerie. Slowly the curtain falls)

About the Author

LUCILLE FLETCHER is best known for her suspense classic *Sorry, Wrong Number,* originally a radio play, later a novel, TV play and motion picture. She has written extensively for both screen and television, and is the author of several successful mystery novels, including *Blindfold, . . . And Presumed Dead, The Strange Blue Yawl* and *The Girl in Cabin B54. Night Watch* is her first Broadway play. A native of Brooklyn, Lucille Fletcher now lives on the eastern shore of Maryland with her husband, novelist Douglass Wallop.